12-21-10

S0-ATK-391

Pacman

Pacman

My Story of Hope, Resilience, and Never-Say-Never Determination

Manny Pacquiao
with Timothy James

"The most accomplished boxer, pound for pound, inside and outside the ring."
—The New York Times

Dunham Books
Nashville

For information about bulk purchases or licensing, please contact the publisher: Dunham Books, 63 Music Square East, Nashville, Tennessee 37203

ISBN:978-1-4276-4768-9

All interior photographs used by permission of German Villasenor. Cover and Interior Design: Mary Susan Oleson, BLU DESIGN CONCEPTS

Printed in Canada

To my dear wife and partner, Jinkee.

TABLE OF CONTENTS

PREFACE

BOXING ICON MANNY PACQUIAO began his life, appropriately enough, on the ropes. He was born Emmanuel Dapidran Pacquiao on December 17, 1978, in the impoverished neighborhood of Kibawe, Bukidon, in the Philippines.

Today, he is known throughout the world as a sports legend, role model, and, most recently, as a congressman in his native Philippines.

Manny is a miracle story. He never dreamed of becoming a congressman or the *only* world-class boxer to hold seven titles in seven different divisions. His dream was to join the Catholic priesthood and serve God. That, however, was just a dream. Born into poverty, Manny never had the opportunity to receive a formal education. He learned from the streets of General Santos City. Indeed, Manny was forced to survive and provide for his family of five in his pre-boxing life by selling practically anything and everything on the streets. He peddled roasted nuts, fish, ice water, doughnuts, and bread. Eventually, he found boxing as the only way for him to survive. Through it all, Manny did sell anything and everything, but never his soul. His core values never changed. Hence, it is not surprising that despite his financial successes, Manny remains grounded.

Many people wonder where Manny acquired the nickname "Pacman." It is the combination of the first syllables of his first and last name—PAC comes from his last name, Pacquiao, and MAN comes from Manny. He has other nicknames as well, including People's Champion, The Destroyer, and Pambansang Kamao (National Fist). But in the end, Manny is just Manny—both a hero and a regular guy—and he has not forgotten those who touched his life. Today, whether it is holiday turkeys or tickets to his matches, he continues to give back to the people and the country that fed and supported him through so many years of hardship. Those who know Manny will tell you that he feels grateful and blessed to be able to give back, and nothing makes him more genuinely happy than to help those who were a part of his roots and early suffering.

Pound for pound, Manny Pacquiao is the best fighter in the world today. He started with nothing and rose to the pinnacle of the boxing world through sheer determination, faith in God, devotion to his family, and the support of a nation of people just like him—people who fight to survive every single day. Now, as a congressman, Manny is ready to lead his people. Indeed, Manny is certainly one of the most influential people in the Philippines; by some standards he is considered one of the most influential people in the world.

He is hope.

He is resilience.

He is never-say-never determination.

This is his story.

INTRODUCTION

I WANT PEOPLE TO KNOW something about me, something that most people did not know: I don't like to get hit. I've gotten used to it over time, and it is a product of the excitement I have created, but I really don't like to get hit.

Let me explain. When I was a small boy in Kibawe, Philippines, I learned that everyone has the ability to create his or her own opportunities, whether through good fortune or hard work. But in addition to these things, I realized that if you are in the business of sales and you are the business, there are two more important things you need: you need to be able to catch people's attention, and you need to be unique.

So when the opportunity came along for me to fight for money, I knew I had to be more than a good fighter who won. I had to be exciting. I had to create a buzz. I had to be the talk of the town, the country, and the world. I remember watching DVDs of one of my favorite fighters of all time, Julio Cesar Chaves. He was exciting. He was a sport unto himself. So I studied him, just as I did with all fighters. But with Cesar Chavez, I studied more than just his techniques and fights. I studied him. I studied the level of excitement that he generated. So, when I started to box, I strived to excite my fans by throwing the hardest punch that the world had seen.

But as I later learned, hard punches are not enough. I realized that I not only need to knock out my opponents, but also need to get hit myself, even if I don't like it. The reason? I need to create a war inside the ring. A war is far more exciting than a one-sided rout. I want to suspend the audience and captivate them—give them something to keep them on the edge of their seats. This is excitement. This is suspense. This is how I became someone that people talked about.

Boxing is a business—a professional business—with deals and side deals. The gym is my office, the ring is my negotiation table, and I am the product—a product I sell to the world. So I am a businessman because I'm a fighter, and I am a fighter because I'm a businessman. This philosophy goes hand in hand with everything I've ever done in my life, not just fighting. From watching rooster fights to observing hustlers on the streets, there's a business angle to everything, and I pay close attention to the business side of things. In fact, even in my quest to become a congressman, I want people to understand that I am a businessman, who has imported a billion-dollar boxing industry to the Philippines.

And that's just a start. As a congressman, one of my goals is to create opportunities beyond boxing for my fellow Filipinos by helping to bring billions more in other industries and commerce. I want to build my country as I have my career. I want to live for my country. I want to bleed for my country. I will bring my ideas to create opportunities for the poor—for the people with whom I shared a path.

I'm smart enough to know that I cannot do it alone. I will need my wife, my children, my confidants, and most importantly, God, in my corner. That's the future, but first, I want to tell you about my past.

CHAPTER ONE

Banana Tree

Clang, clang, clang.

The sharp little hammer descends on the bell, and the sound pierces my entire being. The timekeeper raps on the hard metal at the beginning and end of each round, but this time it sounded different—louder, maybe even angry.

On that December night, as I marched out to center ring, my breath was quicker than usual and my nerves were taut. I was a wildcat ready to pounce on its prey. But this would be no sneak attack. Given our history of business dealings, my prey knew I was coming at him. With his eyebrows furrowed together and his skin folded in, he was more than ready. The world said I couldn't beat him.

My muscles followed my plan smoothly, instinctively. I didn't need to think. All I had to do was shuffle, just as I had done thousands of times before—back and forth, side to side. A ballet of sorts. In just those first few seconds of the fight, I sensed that he wouldn't be able to keep up with my speed and agility. Suddenly, there was the briefest opening. I threw a straight left that slid through his gloves and snapped his head back violently. I instinctively danced to the side. Another opening. He was just too slow to shield the opening, ever so slight. My eyes zeroed in, and half a second later I was hitting him with a hard left hook to the body. My fist crashed into his skin, rippled his muscles, and jolted his bone. I knew he would not be able to take these punches the entire fight. It was at that exact moment that I knew I would win this fight. I would beat the best, the strongest, the smartest, the prettiest—Oscar De La Hoya.

As a small boy growing up in the Philippines, I never imagined, not even in my wildest dreams, that one day I'd be standing toe to toe with one of the best fighters in the world, let alone that I would beat him, or, for that matter, that I would become a professional boxer who would get the chance to try his luck in the ring. Yet I will never forget those early days, no matter what I accomplish.

● ● ● ● ● ●

I WAS BORN in a town called Kibawe in the Republic of the Philippines. Kibawe is located in southern Bukidnon Province, at the center of Mindanao—the second largest eastern island of Philippines. There was no hospital, pharmacy, doctor, or nurse within any reasonable distance of where my family lived. We were poor, very poor, and we lived in an isolated part of our small village. Even if there were medical services, my family didn't have the money to afford such luxury. There was only "less," and I was introduced to a concept of living with less from the first day of my life. As my mother has reminded me so many times, I was brought into this world by a midwife in our tiny, thatched house.

When I was two, we moved to an even more isolated area in the mountains—a place called Tango, in the Province of Sarangani. I never knew why we moved up into the mountains. Perhaps my parents thought there would be more natural resources there for us to live off the land. After all, there was nothing but "less" in the town we lived in.

Tango was a remote, densely forested area about three miles up a rutted dirt road from the nearest village. The jungle was the greenest of green and was populated with every multicolored bird you can imagine. I can still clearly recall how very difficult it was for my family to trudge up and down the rocky, dirt-covered road several times a week to get everything we needed to survive. While helping my mother, sister, and brothers lug the heavy buckets of water and the old burlap bags of rice and flour on the steep road, I loved to hear the songs these birds sang. Though desolate and quite removed from the village, it was nevertheless beautiful, lush, and filled with hundreds of tropical flowers.

Our house was a thatched one-room box called a *payag*, a Cebuano word for a nipa hut. Ours was nestled in a small grove of trees, which gave us relief from the intense daytime heat of this area, which is so close to the equator. It was built on short stilts to keep the heavy flood waters from reaching us during the severe rainstorms. The roof was made of dried grasses woven together, and the walls were made of long sticks of bamboo and other slats of wood laced with hemp, twine, or wood. At night you could see the stars through the grass roof, and you could always tell if anyone or anything was coming by simply looking out the gaping holes in the slats of the hut's sides. If we had lived in a cold climate, we would have frozen to death.

I was about ten years old before I fully appreciated my family's struggles and realized for the first time how close we were to perishing in the harsh jungle environment. Besides food, we had to search for fresh water. If we weren't hauling provisions up the three-mile trail, we were cooking, tending my mother's small garden, and doing any number of other chores assigned to us. I had no concept of toys, television, household appliances, or even a bed that most of us today would consider necessities. My toys were rocks and trees, and my bed was a blanket on a dirt floor.

Back then, my legs were the only mode of transportation I had. Climbing a mountain several times a week was a hardy workout for all of us, especially for my mother. The trails were covered in rock—dangerous and very steep. Now, when I look back, I realize that there isn't a machine in my modern gym that compares to the trek through the wilderness of my childhood. That is where I first developed my strong calves. Even today, I don't have to work on my legs very much—as they have remained rock hard since I was a boy.

My most vivid memory of our home is the large banana tree that proudly took my beatings every day. I don't remember the details as to how or why I started beating that tree, but I believe it all started after watching my first Bruce Lee movie. I recall being struck by the man's speed and agility. I wanted to be just like him, so I spent hours imitating him, punching and kicking the tree. Or so I tried. Looking back, I realize now that I must have been obsessed with fighting even at that young age. Perhaps it has always been in my blood to fight. Perhaps it has always been my destiny.

● ● ● ● ● ●

Clang, clang, clang.

A strong punch whizzes through my defenses. As is the case with many athletes who can put themselves in a zone, I can't hear the crowd, although I can see the expressions on their faces as they wince at the potential of the punch. All I can hear at that moment is the shuffle of my opponent's leather shoes on the canvas floor, and it seems for a moment I can almost hear his thoughts as well.

He narrowly missed my face as I feel the rush of air go by my nose.

A close call.

A fight is a series of constant reminders to be present at all times and to focus every second. I'd become an expert at it. Each close shot is not only a call for further intensity but also an opportunity in disguise.

Instinctively, I step back, this time ducking under his right cross, and then I see a gloved fist whirl in front of my eyes. Leaning into an uppercut that lands on the right side of his jaw, I move his entire body backwards.

Later, a reporter would write:

> *Everyone called it the most intriguing fight in years. That was putting it mildly. The first two rounds went decidedly in Manny's favor. The announcers said it was "shock and awe." There was a distinct sting and snap to Manny's punches, while Oscar seemed to flail and strike air mostly.*
>
> *De La Hoya was back on his heels most of the first two rounds while Manny was on the balls of his feet, dancing effortlessly. In those two rounds Manny neutralized Oscar's left hook and just about anything else he threw. By the third round, Manny had landed more than half of his power shots and Oscar had only managed a meager six out of 56 tries.*
>
> *Though Oscar was taller, he really wasn't*

bigger, and Manny popped and jabbed and skipped around like a jumping bean. By the third round the announcers were saying that Manny was only going to get stronger and faster, while in the third Oscar landed only three punches, and those were glancing blows. Already, he seemed to be lulled into confusion.

In the third round, Oscar became visibly annoyed that he wasn't tagging Manny, and his left eye began to swell from all of Manny's right hooks.

CHAPTER TWO

Catching Fish and Throwing Punches

THE FIRST DREAM I remember having as a child was that of a table of bowls overflowing with food. My family smiled as they ate their fill, and their stomachs were content for an entire day. In my dream, my family's bellies were full and their smiles were content. No one went to sleep at night with that rumbling in the pit of his or her stomach that shouted that we were too poor to feed everyone.

It is true that I could go long stretches without eating, but it always pained me to see my mother, two brothers, and my sister with that vacant and hopeless look of hunger in their eyes. Hunger dominated and persisted for a long time in our lives. I can't tell you how many nights hunger caused me to stay awake into the wee hours of the morning, laying on that dirt floor and staring up at the billions of stars through the hundreds of cracks in the roof. It's the only time during the day when I would let my mind wander and dream. Food was always my first thought, and then I would dream of my family living in a nice home—a real house. It would-n't have to be large or fancy; four solid walls and a roof would suit us just fine. Hunger and security are what drive me to succeed. It is where I get my physical and spiritual power. Even today, I feel that same base urge, as if I'm fighting to satisfy the hunger of my family and my country. Our *payag* in the mountains of Tango was only about four miles from the ocean, which gives you an idea of how steep that mountain road was. I would often walk to the beach. Living in the mountains in that lush jungle and being able to walk the beaches was always a peaceful reward for all of our hard work and struggles. It was on one of those trips where I got my first opportunity to make some money. Though the money wasn't much, the experience was priceless, as it taught me the value of diligence and industry.

I was about six or seven when I met an old fisherman on a long walk across the beach. I remember wondering if fishing would become my lot in life. I knew I wouldn't mind working near the water because these walks on the beach were peaceful and a time for reflection on life's simple gifts. There were several fishermen laboring and dragging their heavy nets from the water. I approached an elderly gentleman who was working hard to drag his net full of fish. He was razor thin and his skin was tanned beyond the color of an old shoe. He had wispy white hair on his chin and upper lip, and I saw that the skin on his hands was so scuffed from the ropes it shone like a brown mirror.

I saw an opportunity—an opening. . . .

As I walked up to him, he completely ignored me, so focused was he on his task. This was how he made his living, and he didn't need a small boy distracting him. If he had a good catch for the day, his family would be fed, and he would have have enough left over to sell in the village. If there were no fish in the net, then he had nothing, and his family would not eat that day. For all of us in Tango, existence was a day-to-day thing. You always worked for your food and water because food and fresh drinking water were very scarce commodities.

I stood by the old man and patiently waited for his acknowledgement. I was not shy because I sensed an opportunity. Even though the man did not utter a single word to me, I waited. Eventually, he nodded approvingly when I asked if I could help him. We did not negotiate for the price of my labor. After all, as a child "businessman," I was in no position to bargain. I took hold of the net like he did and pulled for all I was worth. His look of surprise and admiration told me that I was hired. He didn't expect that a small, thin boy could pull that kind of weight, but my muscles were backed by sheer determination. After an hour or so of working the nets and piling the small fish into plastic buckets of water on the beach, the old man grabbed some of the fish we caught and threw them on the sand. He pointed to them and then to me. I took that to mean they were mine—my share for helping. The payment was even better than a few coins.

I wrapped my fish up in some old newspaper that the old fisherman gave me and then headed straight for the village. I decided to keep two for my family and sell the rest. I asked fifty pesos apiece, and, after selling three or four fish, I went home a rich man. I was so proud and so satisfied. I earned my first real money for my family. Back then 150-200 pesos was about three to four American dollars, and about an average days wages for many poor Filipinos.

Indeed, I was a very happy boy.

Now, when I look back, I think working with the old fisherman was more valuable than the fish he threw my way. Pulling on those nets every week helped to build a lot of my upper body strength even at that young age. My workout plan was almost complete! My calves were bulging from climbing up and down the mountain, and my biceps were growing from tugging fishing nets. A personal trainer couldn't have developed a better program! It's funny to think that even back then my first experience in business was a very valuable one, and it's one that I still carry with me in the ring today. The two were always intertwined.

I threw my first punch when I was nine or ten years old. I was fighting for the honor of my brother and our family name. As I've mentioned, my family was very poor, and most days we didn't have enough money for even a meal of rice. My brother Bobby and I attended the same school, and sometimes all we would have to eat during the day was one banana each. As the younger brother, Bobby would get the hand-me-down clothes. So often times, he was wearing mismatched and unfitted clothes and very worn and uncomfortable shoes to school. Boys would tease and taunt him with the undeniable and obvious fact that we were poor. The crazy thing is that everyone was poor in that neighborhood. So having the other poor kids pick on Bobby shows just how poor we really were.

Bobby wasn't a fighter—at least not then. He was afraid of raising his fists. When he was picked on, he would tell the other boys that he would fight them after school, and then he would run and get me. I was the one who would make sure these boys wouldn't pick on my little brother.

That first fight was not much of a fight, but it was still a rush. I forget the name of the boy who tried to bully Bobby. I just recall the ring of boys who gathered to watch the fight. It was exciting. As the poor kid, I was considered the underprivileged, the weakling, and the underdog. I remember the boy ranted incessantly and would not stop teasing us about how we were poorer than dirt. He refused to shut up and occasionally looked to his friends like a proud prince. His friends would just cheer him on with his every taunt. Perhaps I got tired of his mouth, or perhaps I instinctively sensed an opening. Regardless, it was at one of his cocky "look at me" moments that I threw a straight left jab. It landed squarely on his cheek. Four small white-knuckle marks were imprinted on his face as it snapped to the right ever so slightly. Then all of a sudden, blood started gushing out of his mouth. My left jab caught him while he was talking to his fans, and the punch caused his mouth to clench down on his tongue. That was it. That was the end of the fight. I didn't win the fight because I was bigger. I won because I caught him at the right moment with my quickness. I guess some things just don't change, as I still use my quickness to out-dance, out-punch, and out-think my opponents.

That was just one of many schoolyard fights, but soon as word got around about me, the fights became infrequent, which was fine by me. Don't get me wrong, I never had an issue helping Bobby because I loved my little brother and always wanted to protect him. But it hurt me to the core to know that the other kids constantly picked on him for something that was beyond his control, and the fights were reminders of our plight.

Perhaps, like me, the reason Bobby wasn't a fighter was because he, too, didn't like to get hit. The only reason he would follow me into boxing later was because he saw that I loved it, and he saw how much financial security it provided me. Bobby would work out in the gym with me. Eventually, he started sparring and became pretty good at it. Later, he had his first professional fight before he could even get in one amateur fight, and this professional fight was on a card

I was also fighting on. Bobby won by knockout in the first round. Yes, he too is a good fighter. And although he's a champion, he doesn't love sports like I do. The reason he doesn't box anymore is because he doesn't have it in him to really go to war with people.

Luckily, I do.

The funniest thing I remember about that fight is that I couldn't wear the white shirt I brought with me because my opponent was wearing the same color. Bobby had on a blue shirt, but it was sweaty and bloody from his fight. But he immediately whipped it off his back, and two seconds later I was wearing my brother's colors. Bobby and I had great times growing up. We are really close because of all of our boxing matches and training together, and also because of our shared struggles.

Looking back, I vividly remember the love my family members had for each other. It is a powerful bond that managed to keep us together as a family—a bond that united us in our struggles and in our hearts. Physically, we were close due to our circumstances. We slept next to each other in that one room house in Tango. So sharing the winning shirt with Bobby truly epitomized our relationship, and it was only right that I wore his bloody shirt. After all, we shared everything—including the hand-me-downs that started it all.

● ● ● ● ● ●

Clang, clang, clang.

Freddie Roach is talking to me in the voice I have become so familiar with, even though I hear him every day in the gym and have been listening to him for ten years. Also with me is my closest friend and the man who is second in charge of my training, Buboy Fernandez. He interprets for me in the dialect I grew up with so I do not miss a thing.

I have to take in everything Freddie is saying before I rise up to engage De La Hoya again. My plan is working. I am told time and again, "He cannot handle your speed, son!" I also knew that he couldn't handle me when I turned him side to side to defend himself. *Back and forth, side to side, back and forth, too fast for him to catch.* The plan is working.

Then, suddenly in the fourth round, I go to war with a flurry of jolting punches. I purposely leave myself open, just enough for him to think he has a shot at me. But when he takes the bait and throws a punch, I'm no longer standing there. Before he realizes I've moved, I have distorted his face with a hard left hook that sends his spit flying and the skin along that side of his face rolling up like a series of small waves. I feel almost like I am watching a slow-motion replay. I don't think he's felt many punches like that and I know he is stunned at my agility. I'm like a ghost who is there one second and then gone the next.

The reporter would write:

> *In the fifth round, Manny really stepped it up. He seemed, as the announcer had said, to be getting stronger and stronger. The intensity of his shots was really beginning to take a toll on Oscar. Manny was landing two-thirds of his power shots.*
>
> *By the end of the sixth, Manny was ahead six to zero. Oscar could not stop the steamroller, and he just did not know what to do. The seventh was brutal. The fight was almost stopped. Oscar was hit so hard and so often.*
>
> *Bam! It's the seventh round and Oscar seems to have faded completely. I believe his spirit is gone. Manny throws combinations, uppercuts, hooks, and even an occasional high overhead right to the top of Oscar's head. Half-way through the seventh Oscar was boxed into the corner and Manny's hands seemed to be a blur as he landed one hard solid shot after another to Oscar's face.*
>
> *Left, right, left, right. Oscar's left eye is now nearly closed like a window that was slammed shut. His face is swollen and bloodied. He is going down.*
>
> *At 1:10 of that round the announcer said, "This fight ought to be stopped." Manny annihilated Oscar throughout the entire round. Oscar was slow and ineffective, as though he were an*

inexperienced sparring partner. It was sad to watch. He kept shuffling backwards and was completely confused as to what to do with this man.

When Oscar went to his corner he was a beaten man, and the cornerman tried to iron the lumps out of his face. De La Hoya 7 out of 24 and Manny 45 out of 76 punches in the seventh. The referee was closer to being in the fight than Oscar.

In the eighth the brutality continued, and everyone gasped and wondered when the beating would be terminated either by a knockout or by the referee. Flurry after flurry of stunning blows were getting uglier and uglier by the second.

During the eighth round, I really came on strong. Some would say I brutalized Oscar, landing five or six quick and devastating combinations. His face is swollen, and I can tell as he slowly walks back to his corner that he is a beaten man. Later, the reporters would write that the fight came within seconds of being stopped—even in the seventh.

The fight with De La Hoya was my 46th fight since my first professional bout back in 1995 with Edmund Ignacio. I went from a mere wisp at 112 pounds as a flyweight to win that title in Bangkok into the next division, which is the bantamweight division. I was now at a whopping 118 pounds! After that it was on to featherweight, lightweight, and finally to welterweight at 147 pounds in the De La Hoya fight.

All my life, since my youth selling odds and ends on the street corners, I've always wanted to do something better, to learn something new every day. Boxing is no different. In fact, it was a very tall ladder I wanted to climb, not just in weight classes but in learning how to beat the best of the very best. In order to do this, I felt I had to keep growing—not just physically, but mentally and emotionally as well.

Now, fifteen years after my first professional fight, and twenty years after my scratch-poor existence as a child, I have run for public office in my native Philippines—and not just any office, either, but as a congressman, and I was elected in May 2010.

In the end, Oscar didn't come out of his corner for the ninth round. My idol had quit on me, and I had an odd mix of feelings. It was as if I had called for Superman and he arrived, only to put his cape between his legs and walk away. I was disappointed and even a little sad for Oscar, but overall I was happy I'd won. It was what I considered to be the perfect fight. I had put on a good show for the fans and for my friends who made the long journey to America. It still amazes me that these friends came all that way just to watch me punch someone. I guess we all have come a long way since our days in Tango and General Santos.

CHAPTER THREE

Fighting My Way Out of Poverty

I WASN'T THE ONLY ONE who was reaching for a better life for our family. Some say I may have gotten my left hook from my father, but I know I inherited my determination from my mother. When I was ten, my mother decided enough was enough. She made the big decisions in our family, and she decided we would move to General Santos City in the southern part of the Philippines. It was very unexpected. One day, she just calmly announced that we should pack up our few things because we were moving in order to have a better life and the possibility of work for everyone in the family. "No more hauling buckets of water and bags of rice up the mountain," she said.

And so we moved.

We packed all we could fit into a few burlap sacks to start our new life. Though it is a large city, General Santos is spectacularly poor and rundown. It is located not far from the equator, so it is always hot and humid. General Santos was more of a real city than any place I had ever lived as a child. In fact, it was a bit of a shock to me to see so many people scurrying about, cars and bicycles darting in every direction. My days of roaming the quiet wilderness were in the past.

When we first arrived in General Santos, my family sold roasted peanuts on the streets for a living. My mother stayed up late into the night roasting peanuts and packing them in small bags, which we would then sell for ten cents on the streets. I sold these bags with my older sister, Isidra, and my younger brothers, Bobby and Ruel. My mother's roasting and selling peanuts taught me that there was always a way to make some sort of money. In fact, other than peanuts, we sold anything that could be purchased and resold for a profit. Just like the fish I sold in Tango, I realized there were many opportunities to make my fortune in the city.

One stifling, hot summer day, when my stomach was doing a little grinding dance because I hadn't eaten in a couple of days, I took the little energy I had left to venture into a nearby village. I passed a man selling donuts. I could almost taste the delicious, warm confections on his carts. The smell was overwhelming, and my stomach grumbled as the sweet odor of sugar and fresh dough attacked my senses.

It occurred to me that morning that I could buy donuts and bread for five cents each and sell them for a dime. With the extra money, I could buy some bread and other food. A small business venture was born. My new career as a grocer kept me and my family from the one thing I dreaded the most—begging. I would never beg for food or money.

In the strongest terms, my mother warned me that begging was not the right way to live. Work was our first option. Prayer was the second. Begging was not an option.

By the time I was 13, I was a one-man traveling grocery store. My inventory included bread, peanuts, doughnuts, water—you name it, we had it. Imagine this small, wiry, hungry boy carrying a box of warm donuts down those dusty, hot streets. The smell was irresistible, and I could easily have chosen to eat all five donuts—probably in just a few bites. But I knew if I ate them, I would be hungrier later, and so would my family. I knew that if I ate the donuts, I wouldn't have any money to buy more. I needed my profits to stay in business. The discipline and willpower those donuts forced me to develop have served me well all my life. This was the first lesson I can remember learning: Never give in to your immediate desires. They will make you want more. Later, I learned that this is called self-indulgence, and immediate pleasures could actually hurt me and hurt others around me. Patience is a virtue, especially when you are in survival mode.

There were few areas of town where I would wander without fear. I remember walking through some of the neighborhoods and looking at the nice houses, wondering what they must be like inside. I wouldn't dare allow myself to imagine what it would be like to have my own bedroom in one of these palaces or eat three meals a day in a real kitchen.

My friends said the people in those homes actually had so much surplus food they needed a big machine to keep it from spoiling. They also had a big machine to heat up the food. For a boy who only knew of an iron pot and a fireplace, this was unfathomable to me. There were stories that people slept on thick, comfortable mattresses with several blankets to keep them warm when the wind would blow. The few glimpses I was offered by open doors and windows did not reveal much, with the exception that most of these people had smiles on their faces—smiles of satisfaction and security because they knew their next meal was only a few steps away.

I remember thinking about those things and wishing I could give them to my family. I wanted my mother to be happy and comfortable just like these people were. I wanted my mother to smile all the time and not worry about anything.

My mother's name is Dionisia Dapidran. One thing I remember most vividly about her is that she smiled when she prayed. Praying gave my mother so much comfort. It was something that she taught me to do almost as soon as I could speak. She taught me the meaning of prayer and the meaning of hope. We would all gather together every evening in our one-room home and pray together. Our prayers were always those of faith and hope—faith in God and a hope that He would take care of us. My mother taught me early on to never doubt myself or God. That is what led to my third dream: after dreaming of food and for a real roof over our heads, I dreamed that someday I would become a priest.

I think I must have been about eight or nine when the idea first formed in my mind. It seems even as a very young boy I always believed I could do anything, including becoming a Catholic priest. I knew that as a priest I could one day buy a bed for each of us and I could go off to church every morning to perform my duties for God and the people of the Philippines. But this dream was never meant to be, because no matter how hard we worked, there was never enough money for the schooling I would need to be a priest. I would find other ways to fight out of poverty, to provide a nice home for my family, and to help the people of the Philippines.

During my childhood, my mother would leave nearly every morning to go clean other people's houses and do their laundry. Despite spending her days in this relative luxury, she never spoke enviously of lavish homes, belongings, or possessions. And she never complained about her very laborious work, which could be especially exhausting in the heat of the summer when temperatures soared over 100 degrees and there was no air-conditioning. My mother is the most positive person I have ever met, and she is still my hero.

My father, Rosalio Pacquiao, was a farm hand and a laborer in Tango his whole life—mostly on the coconut farms. He was gone much of the time working in the fields, and sometimes he would take me with him. He climbed the large, swinging coconut trees and picked coconuts for one peso a tree. He got really good at climbing trees and would sometimes climb 70 a day. It was very hard work and took a lot of effort—sometimes twelve to fourteen hours a day just to make about US$1.20, but it was usually the only work available, so he did what he could to provide for his family.

Sometimes, he worked on a rooster farm, and when I knew that was where he was going, I would beg him to take me with him. I loved those birds; they had a distinct air of dignity about them as they strutted in pens made of heavy chicken wire.

It seemed I was most distant from our meager existence when I was watching those amazing birds. Suddenly, it didn't matter if I slept on the floor, worried about food, or wondered how I could ever become a priest. For those unique moments, I would feel as free as the bird whose only job was to stick out his chest and command the pen.

Cockfights are an everyday occurrence in the Philippines. When I was seven I saw my first fight, and from it I learned a few important life lessons. The main thing that struck me was that these proud birds never quit. Never. They never seemed to tire, either. The big-chested, red and auburn birds with their majestic headdresses would squawk at one another, jump and stab with their beaks and claws, and no matter how hurt they were, they would never just lay down to indicate that they had enough. It was never enough. They would literally fight until they were dead.

Such amazing will and determination — heart and skill, I always thought. Those birds truly impressed me and would later be a part of my mentality. I learned then that you have to be quick on your feet, you have to dig deep, and you can never, ever quit.

More than anything else, the move from our paradise in Tango to the dusty, exhaust-filled streets of General Santos City introduced boxing to me in a way that I never knew before. Boxing was something my uncle, Sardo Mejia, had a fondness for, and he loved to watch the fights of superstars like Iron Mike Tyson and Evander "The Real Deal" Holyfield. Uncle Sardo was a true fan of the sport and had a secret fantasy that one day he might train a boxer. He felt as if he had a Ph.D. in the sport after spending endless hours watching fights on television. He would pull me aside, teach me how to make a fist, and show me how to punch. Most of the time it was just my bare hands hitting his open hand. "Son, you need to know this in case you have to defend yourself," he would say. But the look in his eyes told me that based on my slight structure, my best move in a fight was to run — the other way.

When I was twelve something changed my life forever. It was 1990, and I had dropped out of school to help my family sell donuts and bread. I don't remember where I was, but I was somehow able to watch a boxing match with Uncle Sardo. It was the memorable match between Mike Tyson and

James 'Buster' Douglas—the fight that Douglas won. That fight was my first encounter with a professional match. I'd heard that Mike Tyson was a tiger—an invincible, fighting, tank of a man, and I was fascinated to watch him in action. I was absolutely astonished when the grand Tyson lost. My jaw was on the dirt floor. How could he possibly not be the victor? It was then that I learned that even champions could never count on their wins, that they have to earn them every single time. To this day, I still watch replays of that fight because it still amazes me.

Though I was still harboring thoughts of becoming a priest, my life changed that day. I knew without a doubt that I would become a fighter. I knew that the underdog can, and often does, win. This was my first visual hope in life that I could be something or someone. I was the underdog, and maybe not even big enough to be a fighter. There was also the fact that I wasn't from anywhere in the world that mattered, and I had nothing in my background to indicate that I could become a world-famous sports phenomenon. I had nothing to lose. And after watching that Douglas-Tyson fight, I knew I had a chance, and that was all I needed. From that day on, I sat by my uncle's side and watched many boxing matches. My education would focus on the subtleties of the game. I wouldn't just watch the greats, who would become my surrogate master teachers from afar. I would watch any and every fight that I could set my eyes on.

For Uncle Sardo, it was the ultimate blessing that his little nephew shared his favorite hobby. In his spare time he started to teach me to fight, and when he saw I was taking it seriously and that I was determined, he turned his training program up a notch. Uncle Sardo set up a low-cost gym inside his home, complete with a punching bag and some boxing gloves. Even though he had no formal training himself, we both took this seriously and knew that we were going to be champions one day. Why? Because we operated under the theory that the most devoted would be the most rewarded. Pretty soon my friends around the neighborhood would come by to spar with me.

Then we hit the big time in the small corner of our world. As a young teenager, I traveled down the street to the local basketball court which was located in the Oval Plaza Park. While I do enjoy playing basketball now, I wasn't interested in shooting hoops then. I was there for the makeshift boxing area where I could spar with all of the neighborhood kids. This became a huge event for our small town, and hundreds of people would show up with their few pesos for admission. An afternoon of bloody entertainment cost just five pesos, which was about fifteen (US) cents at the time. It was worth it to attend the biggest event in town, dubbed "Boxing at the Park."

I fought at this park for two years until I had beaten everyone, including the much bigger and heavier kids. As I trained and gained muscle, there was no one I could not beat. The highlight of my career happened at the age of thirteen when I beat the unbeatable kid whose nickname was Amang. He was the champion and a couple of years older, but that didn't frighten me. I looked at him as a challenge, and he looked at me as a sure thing. There was no way this little kid was going to give him even a hangnail. In the end, I broke two of his ribs and actually ended his boxing career. (Sorry, Amang!)

At age fourteen it was time to go to new levels, so I packed my bags and went to a city named Digos. Also known as Digos City, it is located about sixty miles from General Santos City on the eastern shore of Davoa Gulf and the southern foothills of Mt. Apo, and it's known as the mango city of the Philippines.

I trained in Digos City for two months, and this was my first professional training in boxing. There were ten of us training there, and we were a team that traveled to other cities around that part of the Philippines and challenged anyone who wanted to box. I guess you would consider this my amateur career.

As a young boxer, I was very successful. By the time I was fifteen years old, there was nobody in the southern part of the Philippines who could challenge me. But I didn't rest on my victories or laurels because I knew I would have to continue to challenge myself.

I knew I would have to grow if I wanted to be the best fighter in the world.

And the world was waiting.

CHAPTER FOUR

From Sleeping *in the* Park *to a* Little Taste *of the* Big Time

FROM a reporter's notebook:

> *A bond was severed when Manny was fifteen years old. Yes, they were poor; they had nothing, but the family did have love, hope, and faith, and those things sustained him. Cardboard "mattresses" and an always-empty growling stomach did not seem such a terrible thing to this little boy; it was even an adventure of sorts for him. You never really want for things you cannot understand or see, but as he grew older he began to realize what they were missing. He never envied others; he was just awakening to all the possibilities the world offered. His family bond made the entire world look almost normal.*

● ● ● ● ● ●

ONE DAY a promoter from Manila contacted me and said he wanted me to move to Manila, where I could get the best training and fight the best fighters. He told me I was good enough to fight all over the Philippines and maybe even in other countries. As much as I yearned for the familiar, I knew that it was time to go. I knew what I needed to do, but my heart was aching. I was going to leave my city, my family—including my beloved mother—and my friends to get a better life. And I vowed to myself that one day I would return to them and bring the world back with me. I told myself that when I was a world-famous boxer, I would never leave my home again, except to fight.

The promoter cracked open the door, but I was just one of his many projects. He told me there was no money for me to travel to Manila. So I stowed away on a boat and headed to the capital five hundred miles away, which at the time seemed like the other side of the world. As I hid, tucked away on that boat, I nursed a pang of guilt because I had slipped out of town without telling a single soul, including any members of my family. Goodbye was not a word I could say to them. It was easier for me to just leave.

When I first arrived in Manila, I was amazed at what I saw. Manila was a thriving and bustling city. For someone coming from the jungles of Tango and the dirt streets of General Santos City, Manila was noisy, confusing, and chaotic. My eyes nearly popped out of my head when I saw my first intersection. There were more people and cars in one intersection than I'd ever seen or even knew existed in the whole world. I was truly a country boy in the big city.

Despite the soaring buildings and the commercial districts, there was still plenty of poverty and crime in Manila. After trying out different spots in the city, I eventually found a few safe places to sleep at night, including a local park, where I made my bed on the hard ground. I guess all those nights sleeping on the dirt floor as a kid helped me adapt.

My employment options in the city of Manila were more expansive than in General Santos City. I was a gardener, a construction worker, I worked in a restaurant, and I was even a tailor. To this day, I can identify the type of stitch on clothing and do a little mending on the spot in a hotel room. I recall my first job in Manila was scraping off rust at a local metal yard, and I used this income to pay for my food each day. It took me about thirty days to finally write my mother to tell her where I was, what I was doing, and to explain to her why I had left. Part of the reason I never said a formal "goodbye" is because I knew my mother would never have let me go. I wrote in my letter that I was very sorry for leaving and that I was also sorry I didn't have money to send the family right then. I was making 160 pesos a day, and I needed that just to survive.

A week later, I received a letter from my mother at the gym where I trained. She was very happy to have heard from me. While she was very sad I had left, she understood what I was doing, and why. My mother told me not to worry about her or our family. She told me to take care of myself and to focus on surviving. She wrote, "Son, the way to survive is to remember everything you have ever learned in your life."

Survive is what I did. Even with a greater pool of work opportunities, my early days in Manila weren't always so busy. There were weeks when work was nonexistent, and on those nights I slept on the streets and had no food to eat. It was just like my days as a boy, except now my stomach was bigger to fill. On those days, I would go to restaurants and wait outside, and even though I sometimes felt the temptation to beg, I never did. Patiently, I would hide outside the kitchen door, in the shadows, until the waiters were finished serving and the managers would come out to hand me food, but I would never accept it without working for it. I would always do dishes or clean the inside of the restaurant for my meal. Because I never accepted their kindness without working for it, most of the restaurant workers always treated me fairly and with respect. I just wish I could remember their names so I could thank them again for supporting me through those days. Finally, my hard work paid off, and I was able to send some extra money home to my family. That fed my spirit in a way that was ultimately satisfying. For three joyously work-filled months, I wrote my mother every week and included about 300 pesos with each letter.

The lessons my mother taught me as a young boy resonated strongly. To this day, I try to teach others to not settle for begging or for taking the easy way out, even if it is freely offered. Always work hard for what you get in life. As soon as you take the easy way out, you will continue to live the "hand me more" lifestyle, and life will only get harder for you. Working for your food and shelter keeps you strong and builds character. This was a lesson that remained inside of me even when I was starving on the streets of Manila.

Meanwhile, I continued to chase my dream as a professional boxer. The promoter who had asked me to come to Manila introduced me to a man named Ben Delgado, who ran a good gym in a very tough Sampaloc district of Manila. Upon meeting Mr. Delgado, I knew he was a genuine person. He was going to take me to the next level. I immediately asked him to train me and to teach me how to fight. He agreed, but as he later told me, he was somewhat suspicious of my overzealousness. You see, I immediately started hounding him to put me in a real fight. Shaking his head, he took a long look at my scrawny, ninety-pound, five-foot-five-inch frame and then laughed.

"You're too small to be a real boxer," Delgado said, but his eyes betrayed his words. I could tell that he saw something in me. In the end, he gave me a chance to take my boxing career to the next level.

Despite my frame, Delgado was enthusiastic about my desire to be a great boxer and the reputation I had built in General Santos City. He also liked the fact that I viewed boxing as an opportunity to help my family, and he appreciated my faith in God. So he took me under his wing and even allowed me to sleep in a tiny room next to his workout area—a room that was six feet wide and six feet long. Some nights, when I became claustrophobic in that small room, I would sneak into the ring and let myself go down for the count. The mat was actually quite comfortable!

● ● ● ● ● ●

FROM a reporter's notebook:

Though it was known as a very good gym, Delgado's place was typical of a lot of the inner city gyms. This was no upscale fitness center, it was a dilapidated building, up four very steep flights of stairs, and seemingly everything was in some state of disrepair. The springs and stuffing of the ringside chairs were popping right through the naugahyde. The ropes on the rings were threadbare. Dust flitted about in the strong rays of sun that poured through the high windows, and the place smelled awful.

It was the first time Manny had been in a real gym, and when he finished walking up all those stairs the pungent body odors attacked his nose. The smells were an odd mixture of sweat,

leather, and talc, and maybe something uniden-
tifiable as well, but he got used to it fast. To this
day, he says he is oddly drawn to those odors and
to the entire environment of the gym. He loves the
smells, and it was really his first home.

Each morning for the next two years he followed
a routine—a very strict regimen. The boy, just barely
a teenager now, would wake up with the sun, slip
on some shorts, and run all over the city. When he'd
covered six or seven miles he would return to the gym
and go through another routine for the rest of the
day training. First, there would be the punching
bag. Then he would work on the small bag. Then
he'd lift weights, do exercise routines, and stretch.
Over and over he repeated this regimen, almost like
scenes from a Rocky *movie, finally eating something*
each evening and collapsing onto his very first mat-
tress in the little room or curled up in the ring.

He never stopped watching the other fighters ei-
ther. Some were very skilled, others just novices not
much better than him, but he learned something from
all of them. However, his two strongest lessons—
move quickly and never quit—still came from the
roosters that he talked about watching as a child.

That what was in his heart; it was his
whole being.

PACMAN

● ● ● ● ● ●

BY THE TIME I was sixteen, I'd been working construction jobs in the morning and training in the afternoons, using my paycheck from a welding job to buy flowers, which I then sold at twice the price I paid for them. I made just enough money to send some home and use the rest to buy food. Even though my diet was simple and minimal, I'd put on a lot of muscle. Overall, I still wasn't very big. In fact, I weighed just under 100 pounds. I knew that the pros started at Light Flyweight with a weight minimum of 100 pounds and a weight limit of 108 pounds. That year, with the blessings of Ben Delgado, I turned pro. Quite amazingly, I got my first opportunity on a weekly, televised boxing show in the Philippines called *Blow By Blow*. The producers paid me the princely sum of two dollars per fight, which I sent home to my mother each week.

I had to cheat just a bit to be accepted on the show because I was underage and I weighed less than the required 100 pounds. So I found some steel ball bearings and put them in my pockets on the day of the weigh-in to boost my weight. I also told the producers I was eighteen. *Then I told them that I was going to win.*

Bluster? Bravado? I'm not sure where my instincts about

achieving success come from. Perhaps from my mother's teachings or maybe just genetics. I really don't know. I do know that whatever I wanted to be, I just envisioned in my mind. I would see it all so clearly, and it was almost as if the thing I wanted was already in my grasp. It's an intense exercise of focus and visualization: I would focus and visualize every single step of what I wanted to be, how I would get there, and what help I would need. Then I would imagine finding ultimate success.

After visualizing over and over the thing I wanted to be, I would then go to work, physically acting out every move, every thought, and every desire. That is where the heart takes over from the mind. I learned from the rooster fights that to be the best, you have to work harder than anyone else. You have to stay focused on your dream even down to the smallest details. And of course, you can never quit. All of this is born out of desire. You must have a passion for what you want to become. I knew there were plenty of people smarter than me, but I also knew no one could outwork me. By the age of eighteen, I knew one thing with certainty: *I would win every fight.*

Despite all of my optimism, there were still plenty of immediate and "real" battles for me to focus on, and I knew I had to focus on each one individually. The first one came in 1997. It was an opportunity for me to win my very first belt. It was called the Oriental and Pacific Boxing Federation

Flyweight Title, and the fight would take place in Mandaluy-ong City, Philippines, on June 26, 1997, just one-and-a-half years after my first professional bout. The fight was against a young man named Chokchai Chockvivat. He was ten years my senior and more experienced, but he didn't stand a chance against me. Knocking him out in the fifth round, I didn't just win, I captured my long-awaited dream—a title.

A couple of fights later, another dream came true. My promoter told me I had the chance to fight close to my hometown of General Santos City. This fight was scheduled for December 6, 1997, against an opponent named Panomej Ohyuthanakorn. I would be fighting in a city called Koron-adal City, South Cotabato, Philippines, which is located ap-proximately 50 kilometers, or 32 miles, from General Santos.

My fight was on the undercard of a very well known fighter named Luisito Espinosa, and I was excited to fight on this card for two reasons. First, this would be my first fight since I left General Santos that would take me close to home. I would be able to visit my mother and show her that I was okay and was growing into someone she could be proud to call her son. Second, my younger brother, Bobby "Sniper" Pacquiao, would also be fighting on the undercard. I had not seen Bobby in years and was happy to hear we would be sharing the same fight card.

Well, it turned out to be an easy title defense for me. Panomdej Ohyuthanakorn did not see the second round. I came out blazing with power punches to the body. Then I connected a good left hook to the right side of his chin. He staggered back. I skipped in closer, and threw a devastating left hook to the body, and this dropped him to the canvas. He did not even think about getting up for the ten count. To make the day extra special, my brother, Bobby, also won his bout. He won a four-round decision over his opponent. It was a terrific reunion and a great night. Needless to say, we had a wild party that night.

I stayed in town for a couple of days and spent some time with my family and friends. One day, I serendipitously ran into a dear friend, Buboy Fernandez, who worked with me in my early boxing career before I had left for Manila some two years earlier. I barely recognized Buboy because his clothes were dirty, his hair was unkempt, and he was smoking.

"Buboy, why do you look like this? Why are you smoking?" I ran up and asked him.

Buboy seemed embarrassed and said that he did not have much money. He was staying with friends, living in one of their small rooms. An overwhelming sense of sadness came over me. I saw in Buboy a little bit of myself. This could have been me if I had not taken a chance on my boxing career. I told Buboy he was coming back with me to Manila and he could help me by cooking for me, doing my laundry, and helping me with everyday chores.

"Trust me, Buboy," I said. "I'll even teach you to become a boxing trainer. One day, you could be one of the best trainers in the whole world!"

Guess what? He did trust me, and today I rely on Buboy about as much as I rely on Freddie Roach, my trainer. Buboy's main job now is to interpret what Freddie is telling me. I know enough English to know that a lot of the time Buboy says what he wants to say and doesn't just repeat what Freddie is saying. Buboy may be my number two in the ring, but he is more than a number two. He has been with me since the beginning, and he understands me in ways that few others do. He is no longer just a student of the game—he's a teacher to me and to many other boxers in the Philippines. I'm sure one day he will win awards as one of the best trainers in the world.

After I saw Buboy, we went back to Manila to continue training. Having him around was like having a part of my childhood there. I was finally starting to see how my hard work was making a difference in other people's lives, and this motivated me to do more.

My next two matches represented the first time I would venture outside of the Philippines to fight. I fought my first bout outside my country on May 18, 1998, at Korakuen Hall in Tokyo, Japan, against a well-known fighter named Shin Terao. This fight did not last long. I won by a Technical Knockout in the first round.

Then, on December 4, 1998, I fought in what was at the time the biggest fight of my career. It was for the WBC World Flyweight Belt. My opponent was a man named Chatchai Sasakul, from the Tonsuk College in Phutthamonthon, Thailand. I won that fight by a knockout in the eighth round and won a world-title belt.

They say in my profession you do not know how good you are until you fight outside your country. I was very proud of my first two outings outside my country, but there was something that happened during this time back in the Philippines that would end up being the most important event in my life.

I was about to be dealt a knockout punch from where I least expected it.

CHAPTER FIVE

Knocked Out by Love

AFTER MY FIGHT in Japan, I returned to General Santos for a short vacation. While there, I ran into an old friend named Reynaldo Jamora. He asked me a question that would change my life. He asked me if I would like to meet his niece. Other than the times when I am training, I love meeting and being with people. So I told him I would definitely like to meet her, and we took a cab to the General Santos Mall, where his niece worked.

When we walked into the shop, I was floored by Reynaldo's niece, Jinkee. She was gorgeous. I was so dumbfounded by her beauty that I felt myself standing there far too long, in silence, but I could not stop looking at her. I was just glad Jinkee didn't think I was weird or some kind of idiot. Fortunately, Reynaldo did most of the talking and suggested that we should meet later for dinner. Of course, I gladly agreed. Dinner with Jinkee was unforgettable. I had the opportunity to admire her beauty, which I later learned was a gift of her Filipino and Spanish blood. Thankfully, I found my tongue at dinner, and our conversation flowed like spring water down from an ice-capped mountaintop. It was pure and refreshing. It was so easy to talk to Jinkee. I did not want the dinner or the conversation to end. But out of respect and courtesy, we agreed to meet again. There was no doubt, as she later confirmed, as to what happened in that store: she knew she won my heart from the moment our eyes linked. She took my breath away by just being herself.

While in General Santos, I could not get enough of seeing Jinkee, and I continued to look for reasons to get to know her better. I was quite the creative suitor. Jinkee was living with her twin sister, Janet, a college student, and her older sister, Haydee. I knew they didn't have a lot of money, a story that I understood. So I would do what I could to help and to win their friendship. For instance, I would sometimes go by the house in the mornings, breakfast in hand, hoping to see Jinkee. But that tactic did not work so well because they were busy starting the day. Almost every time the door finally opened, it was her older sister Haydee who would accept the food, thank me, and then shut the door.

Recognizing the futility of my morning delivery runs, I tried a different tack and started to arrive with dinner in the evenings. This approach worked, and I was able to spend time with Jinkee at the end of the day. Her shy eyes would meet mine over dinner, and her sisters would exchange knowing glances. They knew that the one-man catering service named Manny had quite a crush.

When it was time to go back to Manila, I didn't want to leave Jinkee. More than anything, I wanted her to know exactly how I felt about her, and I just didn't have enough days to do so. I had work to do, so I left Jinkee for a time, but she was not far from me for long because I invited her uncle Reynaldo to join me in Manila. Deep down in my heart, I knew that Reynaldo would communicate with Jinkee, and in this way I would never really lose touch with her. Reynaldo took over Buboy's daily household assignments, while Buboy helped with my training at the gym by holding the mitts and counting my time during training sessions.

After my next fight, which was in Thailand, I came back to General Santos in style. This was the first time I was behind the wheel of my very own ride—a secondhand Toyota Corolla. I was on top of the world and feeling like a huge success. I owned my own car, and Jinkee and I had fallen in love. One balmy summer night, I asked her parents if I could marry her, and they gave me their blessing. When I asked Jinkee to marry me, she shouted a quick, "Yes!" We got married in 1999, and the very next day I had to go to Manila to train for another fight in Thailand.

● ● ● ● ● ●

I will never forget that day in 1998, in a shopping
mall in General Santos City, when I met the man

I would marry, the man I would have four children with, the man who would earn the love of an entire country, and the man who would one day be a hero to the world.

I was working as a beauty consultant for skin care products. One day, while I was talking to a customer, my uncle, Reynaldo Jamora, walked in, which was a surprise—not many men came into the store. Just behind Reynaldo was a skinny young man not standing more than 5 feet 6 inches tall. In my wildest imagination I never would have guessed this man was a fighter, a boxer, and a man of war inside the ring. He looked so sweet and unimposing. His mannerisms were not necessarily shy, because he seemed a bit confident, but he was very quiet and reserved.

My uncle walked up to me and said, "Jinkee, I want you to meet the next world champion," and then he pointed proudly at the slight young man at his side. Manny just smiled a little bit. "This is Manny Pacquiao," Reynaldo said with a big smile.

That was the beginning of what would become a beautiful romance. Manny didn't talk much, but when he did, he had powerful ideas about helping his people and helping his country. That impressed me because I had always worked with the church *and many charities in our community.*

Love came quickly as I got to know this man. I didn't know that much about boxing, but Manny taught me to enjoy the sport, especially when I watched him fight, which was always a love-hate sort of thing. I loved his talent but hated when he got hit.

We were married shortly after we met. We had no honeymoon because the very next day Manny left for Manila to train for a fight, and then he was on to Thailand for four weeks. I was very sad.

I soon saw through his quiet demeanor. He was a real jokester, always pulling pranks on everyone close to him. He was also very charming. He took me out to dinner and brought food home to my family almost every night. It was obvious he wanted to please me and make me very happy, and he did.

• • • • • •

DURING THIS TIME, I was so happy. There was a part of me that wasn't paying attention to one crucial element of boxing—my weight. I guess with all that was happening in my life, I had simply outgrown my weight class. Even though I did everything I could to make weight, including making myself too weak to fight, I lost my belt on the scales. And when I got in the ring to fight, I just didn't have it in me.

Weak and tired, I couldn't handle the other boxer, Megoen Singsurat, who hit me with a quick shot to the stomach that sent me to the canvas. And I couldn't get up for the ten count. This was the second defeat in my history of professional boxing, and I took it very hard. There were so many emotions going through me. I was so happy in my new life with Jinkee, but the sudden lapse in my boxing career was a big disappointment. Now, I look back and realize that I needed this wake-up call.

I came home to Jinkee, and I started to deal with many of my fears. The emotions were raw, and my heart was wounded. I had lost another fight, but my new wife helped me through that hard time. This fight also did something else for my career. It taught me to start focusing on heavier weight classes and on being strong in the ring. From that day forward I started my rise to where I am today—a seven-time world champion in many different weight classes. The lesson was swift and it took hold. What breaks you can always make you stronger as long as you look through your defeat to the victory that can lie ahead of it.

The year 2001 is when it really all came together for my boxing career. It was not only my first real break into the big leagues of boxing, but it would later prove to be my defining moment in boxing. I got the call to go the United States to fight for a world title.

At the time, I was training for a fight in Taiwan. My team got a request from the promoters of a fighter named Lehlohonolo Ledwabe. This man was the IBF Super Bantamweight Champion. Lehlohonolo Ledwaba was known as the "Hands of Stone." I was told this guy was so ferocious that his own managers were sometimes scared to deal with him. A brutal fighter inside the ring, he was just as tough outside.

My promoters and I did not hesitate to agree to the fight, even though we only had two weeks' notice. We immediately got ready to head to the U.S. We wanted to get there early to avoid jetlag, so we quickly booked our seats on the first flight we could get. It was the longest flight I had ever taken—fifteen hours with one stop—but the time flew by. I still remember the first moment the plane broke through the murky evening clouds, and I could see Los Angeles, California, for the very first time. I was stunned by the vastness of this famous city. There were so many lights and tall buildings. I could not believe my eyes. It seemed to stretch all the way from the mountains to the ocean.

Los Angeles International Airport was the biggest airport I had ever seen. It was like a small city to me. There were more people in this airport than in my hometown, and there was more commotion, lights, and people than in all of Manila. Or so it seemed, anyway. I tried to enjoy every moment. I knew this was a life-changing experience.

I remember looking around at all of the different people walking by. There were people of more nationalities here than anywhere I had ever been, and there were so many gadgets. I remember seeing these glass display cases of packaged foods, and then I saw someone walk up to one, insert some money, and remove the food from the bottom. I had seen earlier models of vending machines a few times in Manila but I had never seen so many that were this high-tech. For me, it seemed like the invention of the century.

I managed to locate the baggage claim, where I retrieved my one and only suitcase. Then we took a bus to a no-star motel called the Vagabond Inn, which was on the corner of Santa Monica Boulevard and Vine Street. Amazed at the number of stores that stayed open so late, I wanted to investigate each one of them. It seemed as if there were a hundred liquor stores sandwiched between small motels and larger grocery stores. For some reason I couldn't stop thinking about how much it must cost to keep so many lights on in such a large city all night long.

On every other corner there seemed to be a man or woman dressed in rags. This struck me as strange because in the Philippines, America is considered to be the richest country in the world. *Wow, we as people are really all the same—all over the world. There are those with full bellies and a house. And then there are the rest.*

The ride from the airport to the motel took nearly an

hour, and by the time I got to the Vagabond, I had lost all sense of direction. But I had chosen this particular motel because it was right next door to the Wildcard Gym, owned by a man named Freddie Roach. Before I left the Philippines, my trainer told me, "Mr. Roach catches punches well, and he might be your next trainer—the man who can take you to the next level."

I didn't have much money with me, just enough to pay for about a week at the Vagabond and to buy some canned foods. But the fact that I was scheduled for a title fight in two weeks meant there was a pretty good payday ahead for me. Up until that point, I was making about eight thousand U.S. dollars per fight, which was really good money in the Philippines. This fight would pay me almost twenty-five thousand U.S. dollars.

So in every way possible, this fight was *everything* to me. I knew, no matter what, I just had to make do with whatever I had. That meant coming up with another week's rent at the Vagabond and enough to eat.

A few nights later, as I was running out of food, I stumbled upon a karaoke bar that was also a billiards parlor. It was in a rundown section of Santa Monica Boulevard, and I'd found it as I was jogging by the day before one of my training sessions.

Karaoke was something I knew, so I went into the bar one evening and started challenging people. I also knew how to play pool for cash. After a few nights of song and billiards, my whole trip was financed by Angelenos. But more important than the money I shoved in my pockets after those nights playing pool were the people I met who would eventually make up Team Pacquiao L.A. The Angelenos that I met those nights playing pool and singing would later become my close friends, confidants, and advisors, including my attorney, manager and agents. There is just something special in my heart for every one of them. They are mostly Filipinos, but they are different than the Filipinos in the Philippines, not any better, not any worse, just different. I guess it's like when you have two children and someone asks you, "Which one do you love more?" The only answer is I love them the same. I have to have both because life in the Philippines is much different than the US.

As much as I enjoyed singing and playing pool, I was in Los Angeles to train. The day after I arrived in LA, I went to the Wildcard Gym. Little did I know that I was about to meet the one person who would become everything that mattered in my boxing career. Though my trainer in the Philippines had told me about Freddie Roach, I couldn't have imagined that this man would one day become a father figure to me. He brought a special chemistry into our relationship that I can only compare to the deep feelings I have for my children or my wife.

The Wildcard Gym isn't fancy. It's located in the back of

a small U-shaped shopping plaza that would have fit in perfectly in the rundown parts of Manila. I appreciated that this no-nonsense gym was authentic in the way it smelled and looked. The interior was dark gray in color and very plain, but it had everything you needed and more. I loved being able to walk out of the Vagabond Inn to my workout. Even later in my career when I had money to stay in a nicer place, I still stayed at that rundown California hotel because of the convenience and because I loved to be so close to where it all started.

I soon found out my walk to the gym from the Vagabond Inn was long compared to Freddie's walk. His home (and he could have lived anywhere) was a 900-square-foot apartment right next door to the gym. This proved to me that Freddie loved this sport as much as I did, and he had invested just as much as I had invested. In other words, he invested his whole life.

That is why I felt comfortable putting my life into his hands and unconditionally trusting him while listening to everything he said about boxing and life in general.

After walking across the parking lot of the Vagabond Inn and that of the shopping center that led to the back of the building, I made a left turn, went up the staircase, and entered into the pungent body odors that attacked my nose. The odd mix smell of sweat, leather, and talc made me smile.

Even though I'm 12,000 miles from General Santos City, I'm home.

My manager who was with me, Rod Nazario, walked up to this skinny man who looked like he was about 30 years old. This man had messy red hair, glasses, and did not look like a fighter. I thought, *why did we pick this guy?* I was used to Buboy, a thick Filipino, catching my punches. I didn't know if this guy they called Freddie Roach could keep up.

My promoter came back and they suited me up, taping each hand carefully. Then, I put on my gloves, entered the ring, and stood directly in front of Freddie. I did not speak English at this time, so there were no words exchanged. In fact, there was no verbal communication at all. He just looked me directly in the eyes.

Was that a direct challenge? He raised his hands in the air and nodded for me to start punching. If he wanted to challenge me, then it was on. I started with a right jab to get our timing down. Then I began to utilize my footwork, throwing rights and lefts, in and out.

It turns out this guy Freddie could catch punches like nobody I had ever met. He was at the spot before I could get there. He turned me in directions I was not used to going. He continually challenged me with his eyes and his mannerisms. When we were done, we both just looked at each other with wary eyes.

Then I walked over to my promoter and said, "We have a new trainer."

That was it.

• • • • • •

As Freddie Roach recalls, "Manny Pacquiao walked in. I had no idea who he was. I had never met him before. His promoter asked if I could work the mitts with him; they had heard I caught punches well. After one round, I went over to my people and said, 'Wow. This Manny Pacquiao kid can fight.' I later learned that Manny went over to his promoter and said, 'We have a new trainer.'" It's nice to know the respect was mutual. The rest, as they say, was history.

• • • • • •

THERE IS NOTHING in this world more satisfying than fulfilling your purpose in life and witnessing your own destiny. I knew at that moment, two weeks before the biggest fight of my life, that I would be the new International Boxing Federation Super Bantamweight Champion.

Believe me when I say that we had a serious game plan going in. I was going to kick the crap out of Lehlohonolo "Hands of Stone" Ledwaba. Freddie was sure I had more speed and more power. He also wanted me to go into the fight aggressively and shock Ledwaba.

"Put him on his heels and do not let him get off," Freddie screamed.

Freddie Roach and I trained together for two weeks before we made our way to Las Vegas, Nevada, to fight at the MGM Grand Hotel. My training went really well, and through interpreters we were able to improve on certain technical aspects. Freddie and I had all the confidence in the world in each other, and we couldn't wait to see each other in the ring in Las Vegas.

Since arriving in the U.S., everything just became bigger and grander with each passing experience. Las Vegas was mesmerizing and blinding. It made Santa Monica look and feel like a sleepy town. Las Vegas opened up all new dreams and fantasies. I couldn't help wondering what it would be like to bring my beloved wife and family here to celebrate our victories. I wondered if one day I could bring all of my friends to Vegas to watch me fight for a championship. *Wouldn't that be incredible?* I wanted to share this with all of my people. I missed Jinkee, my family, and my friends.

But first things first, I had to win.

The opening bell sounded and I became another person. There was nothing that could slow me down because I had everything on my side, including the whole country of the Philippines. Immediately, I began my attack on Ledwaba and, after the first round, I don't think he knew what hit him.

Could he mentally recover from the storm of punches I was landing on his body?

I was in a zone and I would not be denied this victory. Part of my iron will was that I was prepared mentally for anything. My vow was just as strong. This was going to be my night. There would be nothing to stop me, but there would be something that stopped Lehlohonolo "Hands of Stone" Ledwaba. A vicious straight left hand that landed cleanly.

I took out the "Hands of Stone" in the sixth round to capture my victory. My IBF Super Bantamweight Championship Belt felt like heaven in my hands.

From a reporter's notebook:

> *Roach had just met Manny Pacquiao, a man who, less than ten minutes earlier, didn't even know existed, but with whom, less than ten years later, would be forever changed. Before meeting Freddie, Manny Pacquiao had already won two world titles, but with his new trainer in his corner, he would go on to win many more—the first of them within a matter of weeks in their first fight together. It was an opportunity that might never have come had the fighter not been where he was, when he was. But in an explosive performance that showcased what would become a familiar style, Manny tore into the*

champion, Lehlohonolo "Hands of Stone" Ledwaba, from the start, breaking his nose in the first round, dropping him in the second, and stopping him in the sixth.

Pacquiao and Roach had won their first world title together, and it had happened almost in the blink of an eye. One moment they did not know each other; the next they were on top of the world.

CHAPTER SIX

Fighting My Idol

IT WAS A HOT SUMMER evening in September 2006 when I arrived in Los Angeles with my attorney, Franklin "Jeng" Gacal. He is affectionately referred to as "Gacal the Jackal" by only the closest insiders of Team Pacquiao. I think he got the nickname because of his shrewdness, which only those very close to him ever get to see. People outside of our inner circle read him as kind and maybe even think he is just a yes man. In reality, he's not only a skilled tactician in business and law, but also very street savvy.

Jeng has always negotiated the best possible terms and payouts for my fights. He and I are very similar even though we are in two different businesses. I will allow anyone to throw all the punches they want, and I will even let them land some punches, but there will always be an opening for me to surprise my opponents.

The Jackal also waits for his openings. He observes closely, waiting for his chance. Then he winds up his left hook. The power I carry in my fists, Jeng wields with his mind and his pen. They are so sharp that most people who negotiate with Jeng never know what hit them until after they sign on the dotted line. As an inside joke, we like to say that he turns my bologna into steak with his mind, and I turn opponents from steak into bologna with my fists.

We were in LA to get ready for my fight with Eric Morales. This was going to be our third fight, and everyone was calling it the "rubber match" because we had both won one previous fight each.

Freddie met us at the baggage claim at LAX, which was a surprise because we were not expecting him to pick us up. The three of us walked outside to a long, sleek, black stretch limousine. I was surprised and more than a little curious about what Freddie was up to. All of the windows were blacked out so I had no idea who was inside, but I do remember thinking, *this limo isn't for me.* And then I thought, *Wow, Freddie really splurged and went out of his way. What a nice gesture on Freddie's part.*

While all these events were unfolding, the back passenger door swung open and out stepped Oscar De La Hoya. My first thought was, *what the heck is going on here?* I had never met him before. Jeng, with his thick glasses, squinted to make sure what he was seeing was real. We both glanced at each other again. De La Hoya was beaming. He reached out aggressively to shake my hand, but I was so shocked I simply nodded and smiled ever so slightly. Then I bent down and looked inside the enormous limo, which came with a flat-screen TV and a row of champagne glasses.

De La Hoya said loudly, "Welcome to my home. Welcome to Los Angeles."

I still had no idea what was going on. I looked at Jeng for an explanation, but he offered none. Shifting from a face of surprise to one more suited to my poker game—a cool, calm expression—I gave Jeng a nod.

By that time in my life and career I'd learned to say little when I felt or knew people wanted something from me. I had learned not to press the action or give any indication of where I was mentally or emotionally. I've found that if people *think* they can talk you into what they want, they will press harder and eventually reveal their hands.

I climbed into the car next to Freddie and smiled slightly. As the car merged into the giant horseshoe that is the inner drive of LAX, Oscar continued talking and smiling. I don't think he knew I understood English because he pronounced his words slowly and loudly, almost as if I were deaf. I chuckled inside and gave him a wider smile to let him know I understood.

The ride took about half an hour. We mostly spoke about my fight with Morales. I told Oscar I thought my best weapons were my speed and stamina and that I would eventually finish him off with a couple of power shots.

With that, Oscar leaned even further into me, almost sliding off his seat. He looked like an excited young man—very happy and lighthearted. He could not control his emotions. He even slapped his leg a couple of times with laughter when he said to me, "Manny, I will personally make you a legend in this sport. Because of me, one day you will take the throne of boxing."

What I was able to read from that short ride was that this was an important night for him and for me. I felt he was very genuine, and I realized he wore his feelings on his shirt-sleeves. In poker we would call those "tells," and they would serve me well later.

Suddenly, the limousine took a hard right and screeched to a halt in front of a steakhouse near down-town. It was a nice restaurant, comfortable, dimly lit, cool, and inviting. The dining room tables were surrounded by ornate red leather booths with crisp white linen table-cloths, each set with crystal and a flower arrangement in the center. Oscar motioned to one of the booths in the back, and we all followed.

The meal was great, and we continued to talk about Morales and the fight, and then, out of nowhere, Oscar reached down to the soft leather seat next to him and pro-duced a large black briefcase. He put it on the table in front of me and popped open the two snaps that held it closed. Fi-nally, I felt, the purpose of this meeting had arrived.

The case was filled with cold, hard cash—a lot of it. It's no secret that I like to deal in cash. I like to keep things simple and clean. I like to pay people in cash and *I* like to get paid in cash.

All of the U.S. currency inside the briefcase was in twenty-dollar bills, and they were all new. I could smell the ink.

As the candles near the flowers flickered, I surveyed the money. Oscar told me it came to a quarter of a million dollars. At that point, Jeng slid out of the booth with De La Hoya and his staff, and they all disappeared into the back near the kitchen. I sat alone, and now for the first time, I could really let loose with my own smile.

Taking a sip of water, I waited for them to return to present the rest of their plan. I didn't know what it was, but I knew I would remain calm when they returned.

Jeng and the others came back to the table with some paperwork. It was a deal for Oscar to promote me and it had better percentages than I was getting with Bob Arum for the Morales fight. The deal covered my next seven fights.

So, they had shown me the money to impress me and then returned with the paperwork to seal the deal. But the funny part was that Jeng didn't want me to sign it. I'm not sure why. But I chuckled to myself, then slowly looked at all of them, one at a time, and quickly grabbed a pen out of Jeng's hand and signed the makeshift contract. Then I pulled the briefcase over to me, pushed the snaps closed, picked up the check for another quarter of a million dollars that Oscar had put under a salt-shaker, and walked outside. It was still hot outside, but I was very cool inside.

This was the start of something big. This deal would start the wheels of commerce moving—my commerce. I already knew Bob Arum wouldn't stand for it, but to be honest, I didn't care which of them won the battle to promote me. I felt that both men would do a great job for me. I also knew that both men cared about their fighters and looked out for their fighters' best interests. So I had nothing to lose.

The truth was that by signing those papers I was looking out for me, for my best interests. I knew a battle would ensue once I took the money. I also knew the stakes would only grow.

Approximately two years later, when I heard that Oscar wanted to fight me, I remember thinking, *hmm, that took longer than I expected*. I knew that Oscar took his business personally. I also knew that when I eventually signed with Bob Arum, Oscar would be angry. Bob Arum, who owns Top Rank Promotions, just happens to be Oscar's former boss, and I had expected Oscar to challenge me much sooner.

Though Arum approached me with the possibility of the fight, he also didn't really want me to take it. He told me, "Manny, I want you to think long and hard about this. I want you to pray for guidance, because this is the golden boy and he's nearly unbeatable. He's fought the best and his tactics are strong."

Actually, the De La Hoya fight was hatched after I beat Barrera again. I was in LA for a Nike photo-shoot with Bob, Eric and Jeng when we started discussing my next three fights. We all agreed Marquez would be my next fight and my last at 130 lbs. After Marquez, David Diaz is the logical choice for the IBC Lightweight crown. If I win against Diaz, Bob said it would be ripe to challenge De La Hoya for a non-title fight at a catch weight of 147 pounds.

The De La Hoya fight did a lot more for me and my career than people realized. The truth is I knew God wanted me to fight, and I knew He wanted me to win. Before that fight, I prayed like I'd never prayed before. If you truly believe as I do, and your faith is so strong it cannot be shaken under any circumstances, then there is no reason to be nervous about anything in life. Faith and confidence go hand in hand. That is why I was smiling—something you rarely see any fighter do—as I walked up the aisle and climbed into the ring to fight Oscar. That is why I was so relaxed. I believed in my heart that I was supposed to win.

Something else happened in that fight. I learned something about boxing and about myself. That night it all came together for me. My feet and hands became synchronized. I didn't have to think about it or work at it; it just happened for me that night.

I now watch other fighters and see that they are not synchronized; their hands and feet don't work as one. As far as I know, no other fighter today has this ability. Every practice and every fight since that evening has been the same—I have felt that harmony in my body and mind. My body, mind, heart, and faith have become one.

A reporter would write:

> *Manny's discovery or gift cannot be overstated. He can automatically, without thinking, take a step back with his right foot and at the same time, throw a devastating punch with his left, all in one fluid movement as if his hands and feet are magically attached. This motion is easily reversed in a split second with his left foot going back and his right hand going forward.*
>
> *Sports writers began noticing it right away. They began talking about it and how they'd never seen any other fighter work that way, including Mohammad Ali, who arguably had the most fluid movements of any fighter in history.*
>
> *Later, Manny scored one of the most brutal punches in boxing history—including all weight classes—against Ricky Hatton. The punch was so hard it appeared that Hatton could have been very*

seriously hurt. Most of the fans around the ring groaned and winced, almost able to feel the pain themselves — like watching a violent car collision right in front of you. And this from a fighter who had fought for years at 130 pounds and was now fighting a larger man in a heavier weight class who could take hard hits and weighed ten pounds more.

Manny's synchronized movements gave his body a completely harmonious balance. This balance adds much more power to a punch because every muscle is working together like a fine-tuned symphony, not unlike the devastating punches of some topnotch martial arts masters that can easily break cinder blocks with a single blow.

The real problem with Oscar that night was that he fought for personal reasons. He had a grudge against me for signing with Bob Arum. Oscar just wanted to kick my ass, teach me a lesson, and perhaps even humiliate me. Like mine, his decision should have been based on business. I looked at that fight as a challenge, an opportunity, and a blessing. It was fun for me. I savored every moment, and when the fight was over I gave Oscar a big hug and said, "You are still my idol." I wanted him to know that I respected him as a fighter, a family man, and as a businessman. I wanted him to let go of the animosity, and I think he did.

Two years before, Oscar had told me that he would make me a legend in boxing. To put it in his exact words—because I remember those words he said so well: "Manny, I will personally make you a legend in this sport. Because of me, one day you will take the throne of boxing."

Yes, Oscar. You were right. Thank you.

CHAPTER SEVEN

Vegas Then, Vegas Now

IN A FIGHTER'S WORLD there is never finality, because no matter what you see or what you do, you know that you have another fight ahead. Until you retire, this thought will always live in your mind. But as a fighter there is a longing for that battle—to be that ultimate warrior.

Edward Lura, one of my top Team Pacquiao LA members, and I took the five-hour drive from Los Angeles to Las Vegas in leisurely fashion. For nearly two hours, there was nothing but an endless sea of sand and rock. When you are winding your way through those canyons of light and energy, you know you are in a place like no other on earth.

The car began to gently glide into the valley. And there it was, like the proverbial Phoenix rising from the ashes, a breathtaking expanse of shimmering towers and glass palaces—thousands upon thousands of lights in every conceivable color.

At night, Las Vegas looks like someone plopped a giant three-dimensional video game down on a moonscape. You are as drawn to it as a small child is to a new colorful, whirling toy. But none of this was new to me, or any of the Team Pacquiao members, especially Edward. They'd been here plenty of times for fights, but even though this was not new, the clock inside my mind kept ticking as it got closer to fight time.

Once we arrived, everyone got out of the car and moved quickly to the action within the hotel, where the shrill electronic wails of the slot machines attacked all of our senses. This was a stealth check-in. I wanted to get to my room quickly and quietly. The ceremonial arrival with the media and public would take place tomorrow.

Edward and I made our way to the private concierge desk where Edward picked up our keys to the penthouse suite at the Mandalay Bay Hotel. As we headed to the suite, any other interests or enthusiasms I had quickly evaporated. The rest of the world was abandoned. The fight was less than one week away. And looking out over the city from my room, I thought back to my fight against Rustico Torrecampo in 1996.

● ● ● ● ● ●

FLASHBACK: Edward and I walked into a beautiful marble foyer in the penthouse suite that could be the size of three homes in General Santos City. I made my way to the window and gazed out. It was not that long ago that I had traveled to Las Vegas for the first time and I stayed in a little motel.

I looked down at the lights and wondered if I could see that little motel from my room. I thought, *is this it? Is this the world I have been chasing? Is this my destiny to bring two countries to battle for the people where there would only be one man standing at the end?* The question was who would catch whom first with that big punch.

It was 1996, and I was on the scales. For the first time in my career, in my twelfth fight, I could not make weight. I had outgrown my weight class. Even though I had depleted every ounce of water from my body and had no body fat, it was not enough. The penalty was to wear heavier gloves than my opponent, giving my opponent a distinct advantage of quickness and the ability to connect with harder blows. I had to take what was given to me and I did not complain. It didn't matter anyway, because I was undefeated at that time and I was not going to lose this fight anyway.

This fight was against a young man by the name of Rustico Torrecampo. I came out strong in the first round and dominated the fight by leading with good jabs and staying out of reach of all of his punches. The second round was no different. The fight seemed to be going my way. I even felt like this guy should not be in the ring with me. I could do with him what I wanted.

I saw an opening, threw a lazy right hook, and the next

thing I knew, Rustico Torrecampo was in another corner of the ring celebrating. I remember thinking, *why is he celebrating at the break? Is it the end of the round? It must be. Why else would he be in a corner standing there?* Then I saw the referee: he was holding me and I could not stand up. The referee was waving his hands in the air and keeping me down. There was a blur around the ring and I didn't know where I was or what I was doing, but slowly it started to come to me: *I am in a fight. I was in a fight. I am no longer in a fight. I lost.*

I later found out that I got caught by a left hook, right on the chin, and I never saw the punch coming. I must have blacked out completely because there is no memory after that until I saw my opponent celebrating. I wondered if this was the end of my career.

Later, when I got back with my trainers and my friends, I was able to put into perspective that I was not the one who lost the fight. The warrior and the champion inside me did not lose. He was still in there and now he would have to come out and show a side I had never seen or felt before. I had to overcome defeat and believe in myself again. All these years of growing up, all I ever did was focus on other people believing in me, and now I had people who believed in me and were pushing me to believe in myself again, too.

It did not take long for me to realize my errors. I realized that I was not supposed to win that fight. I was supposed to learn from that defeat and take something with me. What I took with me that day was the understanding that you need to know where you are at all times in this sport. The truth is, if you do not have enough to offer and you cannot compete at your ability, then you are hurting your fans as much as you are hurting yourself. I learned to not force myself into a weight class I didn't belong in. I discovered that going up in weight was just something I would have to learn how to do. And I would do it to the best of my ability.

● ● ● ● ● ●

AS I SHOOK the memory of that 1996 fight from my mind, I focused on the fight before me—the fight against Ricky Hatton. I knew that Ricky Hatton's entourage was already in Vegas, and he had been acclimating to this environment for weeks. Ricky had left his hometown some four weeks earlier. Ricky, his wife, Jennifer, and his mother, were staying at the MGM Grand.

Hatton had recently said, "The rhetoric of the past two weeks during training camp was mild in comparison to others; it will be a hard day's night for Pacquiao."

Freddie Roach retorted by saying, "It will be a hard day's night for Hatton."

The next day I arrived at the Mandalay Bay Hotel again, only this time it was in a fifty-foot-long bus painted in bright colors with my name, likeness, and slogans. This was the ceremonial arrival for the fans, of which there were hundreds. As I walked through the crowd of people, I was moved by the smiles, high fives, and the love they showered on me. This always makes me smile, and I tried to shake as many hands as possible and say hello to everyone.

From a reporter's notebook:

Later, after Manny Pacquiao's arrival, Manny's mother, Dionesia Pacquiao, arrived. This was her first time in Las Vegas. When Manny's mother checked in she seemed nervous and very reserved. She went immediately to her room, looked out at the expanse of tall buildings and bright lights, pulled her rosary beads out of her purse, pressed her thumbs into the beads, and began to pray.

Later, she commented, "I'm very excited for my son. I have never seen him fight in all these years. I have high hopes. I always pray to almighty God as does my son, so there is nothing to be nervous about."

Her expression betrayed her stoicism.

CHAPTER EIGHT

A Hard Day's Night

THE RICKY HATTON FIGHT was a very interesting one for me in many ways. Perhaps the funniest part of the whole event was the battle of our trainers, which lasted longer than my actual fight with Hatton. And if it had not been for my vicious knockout of Hatton, their battle might have outshined the match itself.

The Hatton fight was scheduled after the De La Hoya fight, and it was one of my most significant challenges ever in the eyes of the world. I heard people talking, and I read the papers. "Is this Manny Pacquiao really that good or is De La Hoya just getting old and slow?"

Prior to the De La Hoya fight, I had battled and beaten five great champions and had achieved numerous victories over top contenders. My fan base was strong, and I had never needed to prove anything to them. Suddenly though, it was like I was just starting out again. I had a new fan base and there was a buzz about the sport that I'd never felt in the past.

Boxing is one of the best-loved sports in the world, but

something had been missing from the sport for years. I felt like those fans and the sport itself were looking to me to save the game. After the De La Hoya fight, my fan base nearly doubled, and so there was an expectation that I would not just win the fight against Hatton, but that I would use it to prove that beating De La Hoya wasn't a fluke. I really felt that I needed to prove that I was a real fighter, and a real boxer. The boxing faithful were looking for someone who could bring back the glory days of Hearn vs. Hagler, Sugar Ray Leonard vs. Duran, and Mohammad Ali vs. Frazier.

Now the boxing world had something to get excited about—the marquee match it needed—and so this fight was deemed *East vs. West*. The battle would have two strong punchers going at it until one waved the proverbial white flag or hit the canvas hard. We would both throw leather until the other was face down.

From the moment the deal was signed, I enjoyed every minute leading up to the fight. What a thrill to travel to Great Britain and get to know the people there. They loved Ricky Hatton. His fans have their own anthem for him and they sing it everywhere he goes. They are some of the best fans in the world, and it was great getting to meet them.

The fight had a lot of personal significance for me. I knew if I were to win this one, it would bring me my sixth championship, each in a different weight class. Ironically, the only person to do that before me was none other than my idol, Oscar De La Hoya.

Hatton had said publicly that I wasn't a versatile fighter, that I was nothing but a hit man. That irritated Freddie, who lashed back, "Hatton's 'Hit man' tag is accurate, because on May 2nd, Hatton is going to get hit man, and hit a lot!"

Before the fight, I got to know Ricky better and I challenged him to something far more serious—a killer game of darts. The game started out well for me because I love darts (and I'm really good at it!). My first dart was closest to the bull's eye, which gave me a slight advantage, but my hat went off to Ricky because he beat me in the end. He is a great competitor and an honorable person, and I knew I was going to be in for a real battle in the ring.

Despite this, I never doubted I had a better game plan and a better trainer than he did. In the end, everything went as planned. Freddie had been working with me on my right hook for years, and using that right hook more often was part of our game plan. We knew Ricky would be focusing on my left hook and my straight left lead because those were the shots in the De La Hoya fight that made the difference. I didn't lead much with my right hand in the De La Hoya fight, so in the Hatton fight we had a secret weapon.

My game plan for Hatton was simple: just keep hitting him with my right until he not only forgot about my left but also that he would have to change his game plan to focus on my right.

Clang, clang clang.

The opening bell sounded and I met Hatton at the center of the ring. It was as if two snarling dogs were circling each other, each trying to be the alpha. No, make that like two roosters who could not live in the same cage together.

Freddie Roach and I knew this was what Ricky Hatton wanted. This would be his fatal error on that second day of May 2009. We wanted to let Hatton assert his strength and be aggressive. When Hatton would do this, I would frustrate him by hitting him with the right hook and moving out of distance before he could retaliate. Our goal was to bring out the "Old Hatton"—the over-aggressive Hatton—the Hatton that comes in with his fists flying and very little defense.

Bam! I connected with a right, then a left, and quickly moved out of the way of anything Hatton could throw back in my direction. This infuriated him even more. Now, Ricky really had to assert himself in that ring, but in his fury, he swung and missed. In his frustration, he grabbed me and pushed me against the ropes. My plan was working.

I remember thinking: *Ricky, watch for my left.* I positioned my body so he would think I was going to throw a left and . . . *bam!* I nailed him with a right hook that sent him crashing to the floor. He never saw it coming. Being a true warrior, he didn't stay down long. He quickly jumped up with a ferocious look on his face and came at me even harder than before.

Now, it was time to impose my will. A right, another

right, and another, and once again he crumpled down on the floor before the bell could save him.

I went back to my corner and knew I was in a zone. Everything was silent. There was no crowd. There was no trainer. There were no cornermen. There was only Ricky Hatton. I knew what I needed to do—finish him.

Clang, clang, clang.

We came out for war in the second round. I landed a right, then another, before ducking, bobbing, and weaving out of his way. Then, as he flailed with his fists, I took it up another notch and let him hit me a couple of times to allow him to impose his will. I wanted him to feel encouraged. I wanted him to feel strong, and I could see the confidence welling up in his face. I could see that Hatton thought he was winning the round. I was building excitement outside the ring, and a sense of false confidence inside the ring.

By that time, I had the fight exactly where I wanted it. Ricky thought he was winning, and I was sure he had already mentally changed his game plan and was now watching for my right hook with plans to counter it.

Finally it was time.

I remember thinking, *come on, Ricky, watch for my right*. I positioned my body so he would think I was going to throw a right—and *crash!* I nailed him with a flawless left hook on the side of his chin. It was perfectly synchronized with every part of my body.

To me, it felt like a battering ram going through a brick wall. Hatton fell on his back, his body centered perfectly in the middle of the advertisement at the center of the ring, which seemed to add even more character to this event. When I looked harder, I could see his eyes glaze over.

The referee was next to him, counting: *"One, two, three . . ."* And then the fight was stopped by the referee. He never did get to ten. Ricky had predicted the fight wouldn't go three rounds. He was right.

I remember looking across the ring at Ricky and seeing him lying there. My first thought was that I hoped he was okay, and then I noticed the referee waving his hands that the fight was over. I immediately went back to my corner, got on my knees, and prayed to God. I prayed for Ricky's safety and I thanked God for mine as well. This was a great fight and the best knockout ever in my career. They called it the shot heard round the world.

After the fight I wanted to have some much-deserved fun. After all, we *were* in Vegas! Back at the Mandalay Bay Hotel, I performed with my band, the MP Band, which had traveled all the way from the Philippines. I love playing guitar and singing with these guys. We owe much of our success to Lito Camo, a very successful artist and musician who wrote my hit song, "Lahing Pinoy." Being in a band is an incredible experience in creativity. It's different from boxing. In boxing, I can hear the fans cheer and sometimes see them stand in appreciation, but when I perform on stage, I actually get to watch the fans the entire time and see their expressions and gratitude for the performance.

After the show, we had a small party with my friends who flew in from the Philippines and with Team Pacquaio members from both the Philippines and Los Angeles. It was a perfect way to end the night.

CHAPTER NINE

Come Hang Out in My Corner

NO MAN IS AN ISLAND, and I've been very fortunate to have many people in my corner who've helped achieve success. One thing we all hopefully learn in life is that we all make mistakes, and we all experience one sort of defeat or another. The key is how you handle this defeat and what you do to prevent it from happening again. I have learned that one of the best ways to keep from making the same mistake twice is to be surrounded by quality people. The truth is, we are only as good as the people we surround ourselves with, both in life and in business. In the military, aviation pilots call these people "wingmen." In boxing we call them our "cornermen."

After every round in a fight, I return to my corner and listen to Freddie Roach. Even the great Mohammed Ali needed the guidance of his cornerman. The reason is simple: when you're punching, dodging, weaving, and moving side to side in the combat of a fight, you can't always see clearly. You can't always see where punches are coming from, and from what angles, so you might miss an opportunity or get stung with a surprise punch.

A good cornerman has a totally different perspective. He can see both fighters as they dance around the ring. It's vital that I talk to Freddie after every round and that I listen to his advice. He's more objective, sees the fight in a different way, and is extremely experienced.

It's the same in your personal life. Who are your cornermen? Are they strong enough to tell you what you really need in life? Do they watch out for you? Are they there for the right reasons? I always tell my friends to have only the best people in their corner. "You are only as good as your cornermen," I remind them.

For me, in the ring, it's Freddie. In business, it is Eric Pineda, attorney Jeng Gackal, and Jayke Joson. These are the people who have always watched out for my business interests. However, Eric is the man behind me in almost all of my endorsements in the Philippines. Moreover, the three of them are much more than business cornermen—they are my trusted friends and compadres as well.

I always made sure that I chose my cornermen carefully. I wanted people who were very knowledgeable in their professions and who could teach me. I did not want yes men and that is one of the most important things I've learned in the business of boxing. Make sure the people closest to you in your personal and business life have the qualities you seek and make sure you can trust them. Be absolutely positive they have your best interests at heart and not their own. Everyday life is a fight in many ways. You need to rely on your cornermen to help you win those battles.

I met Eric Pineda and Jayke Joson during my first fight with Morales in Las Vegas. They are members of Team Pacquiao Philippines. Eric Pineda and Jeng Gackal remind me of my favorite action heroes: Batman and Robin.

While Jeng is the legal mastermind who slays contractual dragons with his mighty pen, Eric is responsible for putting my face everywhere in the Philippines. He is the consummate marketing guy. From Nike, to movies and television, to shampoo and jewelry, Eric is responsible for my endorsements. He is also in charge of all of the paperwork for my contractual obligations to these companies, which helps support my family. I've always admired Eric's personality. He can conquer *any* challenge presented to him if he puts his mind to it. He is fearless. He is my friend first, last, and always, even though our relationship involves a lot of business.

One of Jeng and Eric's most amazing feats was the time they got me out of a very sticky situation. While training in LA for the Hatton fight, a major Philippine network approached me with an offer to air my forthcoming fight on their station. I still had a contract with a rival company, which I was made to believe violated certain provisions of our contract for the De La Hoya fight.

With that in mind, and the assurance that their lawyers could manage the situation, I signed a Memorandum of Agreement (MOA) with them to air the Hatton fight on their station. The news of the signed MOA was on local TV and all over the broadsheets in the Philippines in a matter hours.

After they left my apartment, it dawned on me that I should not have signed the MOA without consulting Jeng and Eric. Immediately, I called up Jeng at around 2am Manila time and told him what happened. He was not happy with the situation I was in so I instructed Jeng to take the first flight out to Los Angeles and bring Eric along.

To make a long story short, Batman & Robin—Jeng and Eric—arrived in LA the next day and immediately took charge of the situation. Eric called up the president of the network where we still have a live contract and informed him of the predicament. The person was very upset, but after much explanation and prodding, he agreed to Eric and Jeng's request to send his top executives to LA to iron out the problem and work out a viable solution.

This time I left it all up to Jeng and Eric to smooth out all the ruffled feathers and hurt feelings. It took another day of negotiations to get me off the hook. When Jeng and Eric finally brought the network executives to my apartment, we just smiled and gave each other a big hug.

My top corner "man" in my life is my wife and life-long partner, Jinkee. She's my rock here on earth, and will never let me forget who I am and where I came from. She will always be straight with me, sometimes brutally, and she always guides me in a Godly direction. She is also brilliant in business. Jinkee owns and manages more than ten businesses in the Philippines, as well as several buildings. She has her own staff of thirty or more people, and she manages every single one of them as well as any top-level CEO in the world. Jinkee has a clairvoyant instinct about the future, and makes all the right business moves. But above everything else, what means the most to me is how much she loves me and how much she loves our children.

One of the many businesses we own is a basketball team. Basketball is one of my favorite pastimes. At one point I even dreamed of becoming a basketball player. It's funny to think about that now, considering I stand a mere 5'6" inches tall. We own PacMan Gensan, a team of the Mindanao Visayas Basketball Association. The team is based in my hometown of General Santos City, and they are known as the MP Warriors of Gensan.

Another of my many businesses is a lottery outlet for the Philippine Charity Sweepstakes Office. This isn't just any lottery—it is actually the charity arm of the government. This means that a lot of the money that is made through the lottery is put to good use.

Often, it's reinvested back into public services such as healthcare and welfare.

• • • • • •

During the last twelve years of my life, I have not only witnessed the change in one man's life and felt a world that was created around me dissolve into an entirely new atmosphere, I have also watched millions of people's lives be affected by one man—my husband Manny.

Of course, during those years, he grew and began to win many fights, and eventually he became the champion of the world in seven different weight classes. During these last twelve years, Manny has worked so hard to become what he is today. If I had to sum up how he did it, I would say it was his determination—he was relentless. In some ways, Manny is still the same person today that he was when I first met him. In other ways he is so different.

Now that he is a famous fighter, people ask me "Jinkee, what is it like to lose your husband to the world, but have the world gain a hero?"

Sometimes, I just want to scream, "Give me back my husband!"

Sometimes I long for normalcy. It is very difficult to share someone who is yours, but the way I keep my sanity is by focusing on the positive. I know that God has a plan for Manny, a plan that is far bigger than being my husband or the father of our four children. I can see now, as I've watched his rise to fame, that he is part of the world. There are so many people in this world who need him. Our world needs hope, and that is what Manny gives to everyone.

Manny also gives people guidance, and he teaches them how to be successful, just like he is. And he isn't only successful because of his prowess in the ring; he's accomplished what he has because he gives far more than he receives. He is accomplished because he's started so many businesses with his earnings and helped so many people with that same money. Manny has the heart of a champion, which is why I am willing to take a backseat to the world.

People also ask me a lot, "What was your happiest moment with Manny?" I reply that it was when Manny proposed to me. I just knew that was supposed to happen, and when your entire being is without any doubt, you know that you are doing the right thing. The second happiest moment was when I found out I was pregnant. It was such a glorious day.

People also ask me what makes me sad, and I reply that it is when he comes home so late because of his various responsibilities. I miss him a lot.

Because of his fame, people are always curious about Manny. I tell them that Manny is a fun father. He loves to play with his children. I can see on his face a total inner peace when he holds one of them. When the kids act up, he has a unique way of disciplining them—he teaches them lessons. He tries to explain clearly what it was they have done wrong. He has incredible patience with them, and, in fact, with all children. I think that goes back to his childhood. He had to learn to survive on the streets. Either his mother taught him lessons or he just figured them out by himself. That is what has made him such a dynamic mentor to children. He tells them to stay grounded, respect others, especially your parents, and know God in your heart.

I have been married to Manny for twelve years, and we have four adorable children—Jimuel, Michael, Princess, and Queen Elizabeth. I think I know him as well as a person can. Though he is revered the world over, he is deeply humble down to the core. He has a natural charisma, but he will only engage people in fits and spurts before he withdraws deep inside himself. Despite his many successes, he is a simple man who likes to live a simple life. He is happy to be with his family and his close friends—that is all he truly needs. In the ring, he is an obvious warrior, but outside he is a gentle and friendly man.

When people have problems or need money, they come to Manny. Everyone in the Philippines loves him, from the important and wealthy to the forgotten and the homeless. People line up outside our home every day to ask for help. They are mostly children, but also people who have fallen behind on their mortgages or have fallen on hard times.

Despite my admonishing him for his generosity and behavior, he finds it very difficult to refuse them. I tell him he is a good man for helping everyone, but he cannot do it alone and he cannot do it every day for every single person—but he persists.

Now, he is funding 250 children in our neighborhood through schools via a foundation he set up several years ago. Some of the children are orphans, others have parents who have asked for his help. He also recently organized the export from the United States of 360 American-built hospital beds, destined for wards around the General Santos region. He's arranged for an ambulance and is overseeing the rebuilding of the L&M gym into an apartment complex that will incorporate a boxing gym in the basement.

Poverty hurts him in his heart, probably because of the hurt he suffered as a boy seeing his family so hungry all the time. He wants everyone to be happy, even if they have nothing. He says, "God gave us everything to live in this world, so why don't we share with others?"

I tell him he cannot make everyone happy, but he refuses to change. It is in his heart, he tells me. "I cannot take a piece of me out and throw it away."

But, it also troubles him that people think he is a god for what he does. I know Manny — he understands people's plights, fears, and troubles. He's been there and nothing pleases him more than to give back everything he's been blessed with.

Although he always longed to be a priest, I know in my heart that he is doing God's will.

● ● ● ● ● ●

I HAVE A PRAYER for all people. Find those who will help you become the person you are supposed to be and don't let them go. Listen to them even when you don't want to. Listen to them even when it hurts or goes against what you want to do. The truth is they can see what is going on better than you can.

I've had members of my own team steal from me. And while it's sad, there is a silver lining to every cloud, and that silver lining is forgiveness. When a team member steals from me, I don't instantly fire or demote him. I sit down with him and have a heart-to-heart talk. If I feel this person is repentant, if they admit their mistake, then I give them another chance—I forgive them. Forgiveness is very cleansing for both parties.

Though he wasn't with us very often my father did leave an indelible impression on me that was different from the influence of my mother. He left our family for another woman when I was very young. But even before that, he did something that was worse to me. He killed my dog. He stole from me. He took the puppy I found and killed it. To a young boy, that was unforgivable—it was stealing something I loved, which is far more terrible than stealing money. He killed my puppy around the same time I left my home to go to Manila when I was just fifteen years old. More than twenty years passed and I still couldn't forgive him.

My father was a part of my early life when I was boxing at the park in General Santos, and he really enjoyed my early years—watching me grow up and watching how competitive I was. But I still held bitterness against him for killing my dog and for leaving the family.

Then, I saw him when he came to the United States for

the Miguel Cotto fight. When I locked eyes with my father for the first time in almost two decades, I was not bitter or mad anymore. I forgave him immediately. Even more important, my mom was at the Miguel Cotto fight and she saw my father. They had a long talk, and my mother forgave my father as well. This was a wake-up call for me. I knew that too many years had passed and that we both had suffered greatly because of one horrible moment in our lives. You see, not forgiving someone hurts *you* just as much as it hurts them. In my mind, what my father did was terrible. Nevertheless, I forgave him and it was like a soul cleansing to me, like a hundred-pound sandbag had been taken from my shoulders twenty years later!

God teaches us to love our enemies as we love ourselves. What this means to me is that we must work hard at forgiving and loving one another, especially those who are the hardest to forgive. If we just love the people who are nice to us and good to us, what have we really done? There has not been much effort. Without effort there is usually little reward. This is one of the hardest lessons in life to learn, but it's also one of the most powerful.

There are times when you're not in your own corner and you engage in self-destructive behavior. People ask me about smoking and drinking. Are they sins? I say smoking and drinking are masks some people wear. Some people use smoking or drinking to escape a problem instead of working through it. I believe excessive smoking and drinking weaken the mind and injures the body. Your mind needs constant growth and challenge in order to meet the never-ending set of challenges and setbacks that life presents. Rather than smoking, drinking or engaging in other forms of destructive behavior, I ask people to take the opposite path. If you took time to sit quietly every evening to watch a sunset, if you smelled the flowers, took a long walk, gave your wife and kids hugs 300 times a day, what would happen? If you took time to help someone down on their luck every chance you had, what would happen? You would feel peace like you have never felt before. You would feel love like you've never felt before. You would feel hope like you never have before.

We all have to take our own paths, and sometimes it isn't the soft grassy path in good weather. Sometimes it's very stormy and your walk is treacherous. But if you know in your heart where you are going and that you truly need to get there, no one, and nothing, can stop you.

Don't ever stop forgiving, giving, growing, learning, and striving. Like they say, life is a journey, not a destination. It is in the doing that everything is possible.

CHAPTER TEN

The Quest for the Seventh Title

IT WAS JUNE 13, 2009, and I was seated ringside with my wife, Jinkee, inside the beautiful Madison Square Garden. It was an incredible night. You could feel the energy as the fans went crazy for their hero, Miguel "I'm No Angel" Cotto. The fight we were about to watch was the Miguel Cotto vs. Joshua Clottey clash. Both men were in the 147-pound weight class, and both were good.

Miguel Cotto was the champion of the welterweight division and considered by many to be the very best in that entire division. Joshua Clottey was the former IBF champion and the number-one contender for Cotto's title. I knew this would be a great match, and I was looking forward to the battle.

My promoter, Bob Arum, invited me to this event in New York City, and I happily accepted. I had never boxed in the legendary Madison Square Garden, so I was especially eager to go there and experience the atmosphere. Plus, it gave me a chance to take a short vacation to the United States with my wife. Jinkee was happy to go with me, and, as you can imagine, she was a bit relieved that she could watch the fight with me by her side, rather than with me in the ring.

I held Jinkee's hand as the announcer began to introduce the two men. She smiled back at me because we were really enjoying our time together. Then, unexpectedly, the ring announcer mentioned my name and the camera operator panned over and showed us on the live teleprompter for the whole stadium to see. When the announcer said my name, the crowd burst into applause. The amount of love I felt from all those strangers was truly humbling.

The love of the fans is really one of the most incredible joys that I have in life, especially when it is unexpected. Sports fans are tough, and boxing fans are tougher. I think it's because boxing is a one-on-one sport that doesn't utilize a lot of equipment, like padding, headgear, or facemasks. As a result, you are exposed and recognized. And the more recognizable you are, the easier it is for the fans to relate and empathize with you.

Visibility is very important to a sport. It's all about how well your fans can see you. The more they see you, the more they can become a part of you and a part of the sport. But there is a flip side to the adoration. When you have such a strong, loyal fan base, they can be particularly tough on the competition. Sometimes they will actually despise the competition, boo them, or make them feel unwelcome. So in the sport of boxing, generally speaking, your fans belong to you and nobody else.

The rumors were already flying that I might fight the winner of this match. I had just beaten Ricky Hatton and I had already fought Oscar De La Hoya at this welter-weight limit of 147 pounds, so it was not inconceivable that I could challenge either one of these great boxers. Here in the hometown of Miguel Cotto, we expected him to win. With the possibility of a fight between the two of us, I expected the fans at the event—who were very loyal to Cotto—to boo me when my name was announced. But that did not happen.

While Jinkee and I were there to enjoy the fight, I also took the opportunity to watch both men and study their styles. As we watched the fight intently, I realized it was going to be so close it might end in a draw. Between the two, I was hoping Miguel would win because he had a great fan base who wanted to see me fight him. But re-gardless of which of these men were to fight me, I would be able to put on a great show for the fans and bring home the title—if that was going to be God's will. In boxing, it's the battle that matters. Your fans will re-spect you if you give them everything you have inside. If you are not the better man that night, they will still re-spect that you tried your best and that you did everything you could for them. Of course, winning makes it that much better.

From a reporter's notebook (The Cotto/Clottey fight)

The Pacman, as he's affectionately referred to, was sitting ringside with his lovely wife, Jinkee, and Bob Arum. The arena was hot and humid; the air conditioning wasn't working well that evening. People were fanning themselves with empty popcorn boxes and the fight cards.

Manny Pacquiao was sizing up the two men. The rumor was one of them was going to be his next opponent. Each time Manny's face came up on the JumboTron, the crowd roared. He was as much of a star that night as the two fighters. It's hard to see how anyone cannot like Manny's grinning good nature.

After ten rounds of the twelve-round fight, it looked very close. But in the end, Cotto won a split decision. I'm guessing the Pacman was glad to see the champion prevail, as this could make for a great next exciting duel between two great champion. And of course Miguel Cotto would now be defending his belt for not a first time, but a second time, against the Pacman—which adds to the history of this battle. When HBO's Max Kellerman asked Cotto after the fight if he wanted Pacquiao next, Cotto shrugged and said he needed a few weeks to think about it.

We've all watched Pacquiao's fights. He is fun to watch with his sort of unorthodox, but lethal southpaw. His agility is unbelievable. Add that to his outstanding footwork, the Pacman has developed a snake-like style, which is difficult to counter.

Miguel Cotto, on the other hand, is a champion as well. He holds the WBO Welterweight title. Unlike Pacquiao, Cotto has power on his side and a "naturally" larger physique, whereas there were still questions about whether Pacman could bring his power up to yet another weight class? Will he lose some of that power or speed as he has to work hard just to get up to the weight of 147? 147 pounds doesn't come naturally to Manny, though he did beat De La Hoya handily at that weight. Manny actually had to force himself to eat extra meals and sometimes had to curtail his training to retain his calories and maintain his weight.

Ah, the debate will continue. Cotto is a natural welterweight. He has the home court advantage, so to speak. Given that alone, Team Pacquiao should, in people's opinions, not take this fight lightly. Cotto will bring everything he's got to keep his title. However, as the debate rages and the bets start piling up in Vegas, Pacquiao is in his prime, so the home court might not be as much of an advantage.

To win this fight, Cotto has to play it smart. He might learn a few things from Marquez, who the Pacman had a difficult time beating. Cotto will also have to time his punches correctly or he'll waste a lot of energy chasing the ghost around the ring.

Pacquiao will probably be favored when all is said and done, though Cotto would be his toughest test to date. The Pacman, it must be pointed out, has already beaten men this size, so he's used to it. His biggest advantage is neither his speed nor his growing strength (given that punch heard round the world to Ricky Hatton's head), but it will be his amazing boxing IQ. He's got all the weapons in his toolbox that he needs.

In order to win, he just has to be himself.

The minute Miguel Cotto won the fight I immediately began to visualize fighting him. Miguel is a warrior, a champion, and that excited me even more. I told Bob Arum I wanted to fight Miguel Cotto, and I asked him to make it happen. Sure enough, within a couple of months, the fight was inked.

By that time I was busy with other things. I was filming a movie called *Wapakman,* and working on my TV show, *Show*

Me Da Manny. These commitments kept me from training. My fans began to pressure me to begin training, but I never start seriously until eight weeks out from any fight.

When the magic day came (two months out), we did not have a place to train. I didn't want to work out in Los Angeles because being in the U.S. for that long would put me in a much higher tax bracket, but no one on my staff could find another location. Finally, I decided to just stay in the Philippines and settle in a place called Baguio.

To prepare for Cotto, I focused on building strength and mass, while mentally concentrating on Cotto's weaknesses and strengths. Just days after that decision, my beloved country was hit by a horrendous storm, which devastated the Philippines, and in particular, Baguio and Manila. So many people were left homeless, dead, or injured, and it was hard for me to focus on my training. I thought long and hard about whether to get involved with rescue work or to remain centered on the task in front of me. I prayed for guidance, and eventually my prayers were answered. The answer? Stay focused on this fight. Stay focused on Cotto. If you do, you will be able to help your country in a much bigger way. You'll be able to bring back money and more world support to your entire country.

I continued to train, but one of my favorite aspects of training—running—was made nearly impossible for the condition of the area. So, my team had to create another way for me to build endurance and stamina, and they decided swimming would be the next best option.

That didn't go over well with me. I hate swimming. I don't, and can't, relate to fish—roosters perhaps, but not fish. I have very little body fat, and I don't float too well. I swallow water, cough, and struggle most of the time I'm in the water.

Luckily, Freddie Roach was not the only one from my team who showed up to help me train for Cotto. Freddie brought Alex Arizza with him. Alex is my strength and conditioning coach, and he saved me during these tough times. Alex is a great swimmer, and he got in the water with me and forced me to do what I did not want to do. Alex just seems to have the ability to push me to higher levels in everything we do. He found new exercises and new ways to make me stronger and faster, and he is one of the main reasons I was able to dominate De La Hoya, knock out Hatton, and grow stronger than Cotto, who was supposed to be the bigger, stronger man.

As time continued, I got in some great workouts in Baguio. But there was tension in my camp, which isn't always a bad thing in my eyes. I view it as a sign of passion. It means they are putting their emotions into their jobs and that they care about the responsibilities.

One day, Freddie's strength coach got into a fistfight with my Advisor, but I didn't take it seriously. I mean, we are all grown men and those things happen. I'd be more worried if it didn't happen. When you put that many different personalities in a tight space day after day after day, "disagreements" are bound to bubble up. I normally stay away from this type of drama by doing my own thing. I never found out exactly what happened, but one thing was for sure: even though I was relaxed and focused, my team was tense. They wanted me to take Cotto's belt.

When I was not training with Freddie in our gym, I played basketball. We had a very nice indoor court where we were staying—and it was dry. Playing basketball was a very fun way for me to get my cardio in while getting everything off of my mind. It was also a time for me to discuss politics and get ready for another run at being a politician. I had run for a seat in the House of Representatives in the May 2007 legislative election, hoping to represent the first District of South Cotabato, but was defeated by my incumbent opponent.

Finally, it was time to leave Baguio for Manila. I spent about three days in Manila—a mental vacation before traveling to Los Angeles. It was also a time for me to get closer to the tragedy of Typhoon Ondoy that hit Manila so hard. When I arrived in Manila, I saw so many people in good spirits—it was very encouraging. I also learned that the charity I had set up was having a positive impact on the relief efforts. As a result, I was able to enjoy my time during those three days in Manila, but this did not sit well with Freddie Roach. With Freddie, there was no room for distractions. He could see that I had other things on my mind. It must have shown in the gym. I agree with him that I was distracted in Manila, but I felt confident in the work we did in Baguio, and I felt ready to fight Miguel right then and there. The truth is, I needed to know that Manila and my people were okay.

Three weeks before the fight, I flew to Los Angeles to meet with Team Pacquiao L.A. As I was flying over Los Angeles, I remembered my very first trip to the United States back in 2001. Wow, how things had changed since then. But while looking at all of those lights, I reflected on how the beautiful things in my life were still the same, just as these beautiful lights were still the same.

When the plane touched down, I was greeted by my friend and my personal bodyguard, Rob Peters. He is very quick on his feet for a big guy, and, most importantly, he understands that I have to interact with my fans. Rob greeted me with a huge smile. We were both happy to see each other, but he also had a serious look on his face. We knew how close we were to the upcoming fight.

Rob escorted me through a warm and boisterous reception at the Los Angeles International Airport—the largest welcome I had ever received. After saying hello to my fans, I drove to my apartment in Hollywood—a condominium known as the Palazzo. We were going to train these last few weeks in L.A. at the Wildcard Gym before the trip to Vegas for the upcoming fight.

Training picked up in the Wildcard Gym right where we left off when I was in Baguio, Philippines. Sometimes when Freddie would hold up the mitts during practice, I would hit his hands so hard that the mitts would go flying off. There were also times in training were Freddie would make me stop even though I wanted to keep going. So Freddie would hold up his mitts again and I would pound away as hard as I could with combinations. Freddie's mitt went flying, and he said, "Manny, that's it. He's out. The fight is over. He is done."

This was the strongest I had ever felt. I felt like I still had my speed, and I knew conditioning would not be any concern at all because I was able to run every single day. Everything was coming together.

Apart from my training during these three weeks, I spent some time setting up my personal website: mpboxing.com. I was truly excited about the effort because it would allow me, for the first time, to communicate with my fans directly. It gave them a chance to see me up close and personal—all of the facets of my career and personality. I think it is important for the world to see what you are doing and the good ways you are trying to help your countrymen. I believe and hope it will motivate others to do the same.

In many ways, life seemed to really be coming together for me on an international basis. Broadcasting to the world was a thrill, and I began to realize the impact this medium could have in my efforts to reach out to my countrymen. The Internet is a wonderful place.

One nice thing about moving up in weight class was that I could finally eat a lot of good food right before every workout. When I was fighting at those lower weight classes, I could not eat as much as I wanted. I had to diet just to make weight. I was never at my full strength when I fought in those lower weight classes, but when I fought Oscar De La Hoya, Ricky Hatton, and Miguel Cotto, I never felt better. I was strong and full of energy and power. Perhaps I was suited to fight at this weight class.

From a reporter's notebook:

As with most fights of this caliber that are this anticipated, tensions run high in training and across the two camps. Freddie Roach fired the first volley with his put-down of Cotto's trainer, his counterpart, Joe Santiago, by saying, "I'm unimpressed with Santiago. There is a lot of green in Cotto's corner."

It doesn't take much to rub a situation the wrong way, and that started the war of words, which for promoters isn't a bad thing. Any talk that escalates the interest of the fans is good. Any trash talking between the fighters also fuels the marketing fire and cable revenues. It also gives the media, which is ravenous for any new information, the sound bites and visual material we thirst for.

The last week of training before the fight, Bob Arum visited Cotto's gym and declared, "Miguel Cotto is better today than ever before."

As the weeks drew closer to the actual fight, promoters like Arum and others would often dream up very creative ideas to keep the interest as hot as possible. One such event was held a couple of nights before the fight at the Ricardo Montalban Theater in Hollywood. Neither fighter would travel to Vegas until two days before the event. At the Montalban, Manny Pacquiao and a few others on stage answered questions from the event manager. The first question to Manny was, "What does it mean to you to be number one in the world?" Manny answered in his traditional humble manner: "It means I give thanks to my fans. They are the ones who have made me number one. It means, 'thank you.'"

Continuing the hype, glamour, and excitement just prior to the fight, celebrities began pouring into the gym in Hollywood where Manny was wrapping it all up.

First, there was Sly Stallone, the one-and-only Rocky Balboa, who teased Freddie Roach in the lobby by telling him and the huddle of sports reporters, "I'll tell you what, this is the best trainer and fighter in the world today. I would not want to get into the ring with Manny."

Next came Mickey Rourke, who brought with him a recent cover of TIME *magazine that featured a tight headshot of Manny. Showing it to Roach, he declared him not only the best trainer, but also the best promoter for his fighter.*

Later, Wayne Newton, Mr. Las Vegas, said, "Anything you can imagine can happen here in Las Vegas and that holds true for this fight." And he would know. Newton has been a favorite performer and resident of this sprawling desert megacity for more than thirty years.

The already crazy, high-energy buzz that Vegas exudes is always raised up a notch or two when there's a big fight in town. Pacquiao vs. Cotto was no exception. It was one of the most anticipated fights of 2009 with the possible exception of the Pacquiao/De La Hoya match up.

Indeed, the city takes on a heightened vigor and even a bit of chaos just prior to a fight like this one. The sports books report a frenzy in betting similar to other major sporting events, such as the Super Bowl, the NBA Finals and March Madness.

Millions and millions of dollars exchange hands legally in Vegas and illegally all over the rest of the world. It is impossible to guess at the overall number, but it is huge.

Cotto is one and one-half inches taller than Manny but only one pound heavier than him. As Michael Buffer begins the announcements, a quick scan of the arena at the MGM Grand reveals that it is packed. Thousands wait in anticipation, and millions upon millions more are watching on HBO's Pay-Per-View.

After his ritual prayers and last-minute talk with Freddie Roach, Pacquiao appears between the stands wearing his traditional blue and red satin robe. He is smiling as he pumps his red gloves together trying to begin to get the feeling of contact. He looks very relaxed.

Getting into the ring on the opposite side is Miguel Cotto, wearing an all-white robe with hood pulled way down almost over his eyes. Before the fight, Freddie Roach has issued a final statement: "Tonight's fight will be a repeat of the De La Hoya fight—a wipeout and over fast."

Not everyone is so sure of that. Cotto is very strong, and some say just as fast as Pacquaio, and he can take the punches. What is going to happen when Pacquiao gets hit repeatedly by a stronger and taller, natural welterweight? That is what the boxing world wants to know.

I was about to take the ring for the chance to add my seventh championship belt in seven different weight classes, which would break the world record held by none other than Oscar De La Hoya.

Miguel Cotto, they all said, was bigger and stronger, but I felt I was smarter and faster, and heart has as much—or more—to do with it than just strength and quickness. I know how big my heart is, so my strength and agility in this fight would not be an issue.

Our game plan was to go to war with Cotto. I really wanted to give the fans a good back-and-forth battle, unlike what I'd done with Oscar De La Hoya, where I was too fast to be hit. I wanted a war with Miguel Cotto, and I wanted to show my fans and his fans how much the heart can overpower anything you have in front of you. So I allowed Cotto to hit me. I wanted to show him he couldn't hurt me. I hoped this would break his spirit a little bit, but even though I tried to show him I was not hurt, I really was pretty banged up. Cotto hurt me with some of his powerful shots, and he even busted my eardrum in the third or fourth round.

I kept fighting anyway.

ROUND ONE

Clang, clang, clang.

We both came out swinging. Cotto was the first to land a shot. It was a hard jab that tagged me on the chin. My head snapped back.

I could see quickly that he wanted to fight in close to avoid my deadly mid-range shots. I also realized I would have to give this man more respect than I did Oscar or Ricky Hatton.

After several exchanges—none of which hurt either of us—I heard the familiar "click, click, click," which signaled only ten seconds left in the round. I felt that Cotto had won the first round, even though officially we had both landed twelve punches. Some of his were real power punches.

ROUND TWO

IN THE SECOND ROUND, I came out more aggressively. Cotto was a good counter-puncher and he got in a good leading left jab on me. At one minute and 33 seconds, I opened up a blistering volley of combinations, most of which struck their targets. I was just too fast for him, though he was almost just as quick. I sensed the round was a draw, but maybe they would give it to Cotto.

ROUND THREE

IN THE THIRD ROUND, Cotto got in a good left hook right away, immediately followed by a strong shot to my belt. The referee warned him, but he hadn't caught me low enough to do any real damage.

Suddenly, *bam, bam, bam!* I let loose, stunning him with three hot lefts. I then began to ratchet the fight up a few notches. My hands were moving so fast that even I couldn't clearly see them. I was landing lots of combinations and jabs, but they didn't seem to be backing him up. The man could really take a shot.

Now, we were trading punches, shot for shot. It was an all-out war. They said it looked like spontaneous combustion when I threw several combinations in a row. I was coming at him from weird angles, which confused him a little, and suddenly, I saw a slight opening. I threw a hard right hook and Cotto went down on all fours, but he wasn't out. When he got up again, we started trading punches once more. I was using my jab more and he was using his right and going to the body more. And then, *boom, we butted heads*—which always hurts, but there was no blood on either of us. Just as suddenly, he caught me with an uppercut that stunned me and backed me up. I didn't know it at the time, but they had me two to one after that round. The referee had given me an extra point for the knockdown.

ROUND FOUR

IN THE FOURTH ROUND, I felt that anything could happen in the blink of an eye, but Cotto was being more defensive and protecting against another quick knockdown. I delivered three quick shots and then he responded by tagging me on the chin with a right. It was a good blow. A minute and a half into the round, I decided to take a short breather and do the unthinkable—something that worried Freddie a great deal. Lying on the ropes, I allowed Cotto to take body shots. I covered up my face and just let him pound away for about ten seconds. I knew Freddie was screaming for me to get off the ropes, but I was okay. Then, as if to signal to both Cotto and Freddie, I raised my arms and tapped my gloves together as if to say, "Come on. Is that all you have?"

The sweat was literally washing over both of us as we reengaged at center ring. Then, suddenly, with 17 seconds left in the round, I let loose with a beautiful left hook and Cotto went down on all fours again. He was stunned and angry because I knew he had the round won until I got that extra point.

ROUND FIVE

THERE HAD BEEN four incredible rounds so far. I was giving the fans what they wanted—a war. In the beginning of this round, my jab was working well. Then I let loose with a flurry of lefts and rights, mostly to Cotto's face and head. I could tell he was slowing down, but I was speeding up. This round was not as violent as the fourth round except for the late left hook he caught me with.

ROUND SIX

IN THE SIXTH ROUND, Cotto seemed to slow down, and I wondered if I could finish him, but in boxing this is not something you can focus on or build your game plan around. You just need to fight your fight and accept the openings given to you or the ones that you create. You really are only concerned with finishing your opponent once you have him hurt or stunned, or maybe when you break his will to fight.

I could tell Cotto didn't have much in him anymore, but he was a warrior and a true champion. Even though he was tiring, he got me with a good right hook. I promptly returned the favor with a stiff one to his face. Toward the end of the round, I caught him with a great left hook and he nearly went down again, but braced himself holding onto the rope with his left hand. I grinned and walked away.

ROUND SEVEN

AT THIS POINT, the scorers had the fight 58 to 54 in my favor, though, at the time I wasn't aware of it. I was now putting Cotto where I wanted him even more than in the beginning of the fight. *Bam, bam, bam, bam.* I sent out a fusillade of rights and lefts—more than ten shots in about five seconds. At this point I realized it was just a matter of time. He wasn't attacking anymore.

ROUND EIGHT

QUICKLY, I get in a hard right punch. Cotto could take punches, but now those who questioned my ability against a "natural" welterweight could see that I was better at this weight class because the extra calories gave me more energy and strength.

He hit me with a stiff right and cut my eye, but then I turned him around and got him on the ropes, where I landed several combinations. I wanted to finish him, but he wasn't going to quit. This was very apparent to me now.

ROUND NINE

WE WERE A MINUTE and forty seconds into the ninth round, and he was in big trouble. He couldn't even see my punches coming. Then I went for it. I knew I could finish him, and to that end I hit him with a straight right that felt almost as hard as the Hatton punch. Still, he didn't give up. His face was swollen beyond belief, and I could feel my face starting to swell. This was what everyone was hoping for—and what I had trained for those past few weeks. This was my moment.

Speed kills, I thought. But like the roosters, if he never quits, he might go the distance. I didn't want that to happen, so I continued to pummel him.

ROUND TEN

I REALLY WANTED to take him out, and the time was now. Stalking him like a hungry mountain lion as he backed up, I looked at my prey. Later, the writers declared that Cotto wanted to go out on his own terms. He didn't want the fight stopped, but at that moment his terms were painful. I thought he would go down. I was amazed at his determination and perseverance. I've fought few men like him, and I've known others to take the punches he took, only to fall and not get back up. Miguel Cotto was earning my respect more and more with each round he was losing.

ROUND ELEVEN

I CAME OUT FAST and aggressive in round eleven. The murmur in the crowd rumbled of high expectations, and I knew the crowd was itching for me to end this fight. There were a lot of Pacman fans there, and most of them had flown in from the Philippines and wanted me to press the fight. I remembered hitting Freddie's mitts and watching them go flying off his hands. I remembered Freddie say, "It's over Manny. He's out!" But Miguel was still in front of me. He was not out, which meant I needed to work harder.

Throwing twenty punches in quick succession, I tried to close the door. But I was also bleeding from a cut over my left eye and he was bleeding from the one over his right eye. My hands were swollen inside my gloves, and one of them had so much pain radiating from it that I feared it was broken. I knew my eardrum had been broken in the third or fourth round. This was a brutal war and I had the battle scars to prove it.

Now, there was only a minute left and he was in full retreat. I kept chasing him, trying to engage him. Suddenly, he was on the ropes again. I had trapped him and he couldn't dance or retreat. He was only running on pride.

ROUND TWELVE

THERE WAS ONLY the last round. Could he make it? Chasing, chasing, chasing. *Is he going to fight me?* I thought, looking at Kenny Baliss, the referee. Later, I was told that Cotto's father, in his corner, had begged him to stop the fight. Miguel said no. I was thinking the same thing and then I knew what I needed to do, so the last twenty-five seconds were a vicious smothering of Cotto with a machine-gun intensity of shots from my arsenal.

Suddenly, I got through. I hit Miguel with such a hard left hook that it went right through his gloves and caught him on the right side of his face. I knew this had to be it.

I saw him crashing back into the ropes. I knew for sure the fight was over and he wouldn't be able to handle my next punch, so I moved in for the finish, and at the same instant, the referee stepped in and saved Cotto from any more punishment. I had stopped him in the last round. I was given a TKO by being stronger than Miguel Cotto, the person the world said would be too strong for me.

With this fight, I had wanted to prove to the world, to my fans, and to the children in the streets that they only need heart to make it through tough times. Sometimes, that is all you need, sometimes that is all you have—just your heart. This cannot be measured by statistics, or what others tell you. Nor can it be measured by the opinions of others. It is what it is. It takes everything you have inside to just make it happen, no matter what.

CHAPTER ELEVEN

A Typical Night in the Life of Pacman

WHAT PEOPLE WOULD probably find most interesting about me is that in my everyday life I use the same in-and-out movement that you see in the ring. It is important for me to be as unpredictable outside the ring as I am inside. Whether it's in business, or on the tough city streets, I have to handle the life that has been created around me.

People tell me I have more energy than anyone they have ever met. I keep my team on their toes, usually until all hours of the night, and then I am up early the next day to do it again. If you want to do business with me, or be a part of my team, you have to be prepared to keep up and handle my movements—and not many can.

You see, on the streets, everything is a hustle. It is all about survival and how good your game is. It doesn't matter if your game is billiards, darts, or selling donuts, the key is, *how good are you*? Will you survive? I love the streets because that is where you can feel the heart of the people. It is the soul of the city. The inner city is the air, and the hustle is my oxygen.

This part of my life allows me time to relax. My mind is removed from the decisions that will directly impact so many lives. It is a time for me to unwind and not have to think about taking care of people, though I constantly worry about them anyway.

I see their faces in my mind, and those expressions fuel me. The hungry children, the old, wrinkled, pained elders, or babies that have no mother or father. Thinking about these people fuels me and keeps me passionate about everything I am. It's the reason I will never change.

Crack . . .

I hear the sound of the balls breaking apart. That sound releases me to focus on what I need to do. I make the break for the opening game, and I watch the cue ball bounce off the rail and back in my direction to the center of the table. I am ready to put the next colored ball in the corner pocket.

This scene is vastly different than the one I was a part of just two hours earlier when I was dining with the former president of the Philippines and his son. There was sushi-grade tuna caught earlier the same day along with the finest and freshest vegetables and fruits available. Batman and Robin (Jeng and Eric) were there. They are two of the few who can keep up with me.

We arrived a few minutes late and were escorted into a dining area. There were great wines and cheeses, and the conversation was stimulating. The first thing the former president tells me is, "Manny, you know that you are a savior to our people. You broaden their sense of the world outside of the Philippines. You give your people hope." I thanked him and smiled.

The Filipino people have a lot of pride. For the former president to say this to me only adds to my belief that I am doing what I was placed on this earth to do. People need hope. With hope, we can get through what we have in front of us today and press forward until tomorrow. Hope is as important as love because without one you can't have the other. It is through hope, love, and the understanding of our purpose in life that we create happiness in ourselves and become the person God intended us to be.

The power I possess comes from deep inside. It comes with the synchronization that God has bestowed upon me. It comes with the hours of training that have been going on for years. It comes with the glory that I have found in victory. The power I possess also comes from love and from hope.

There is an irony in the fact that I am able to instill hope in people through my profession of boxing, which some view as one of violence—a fighter willing to go to war with anyone at any time. It has been said by ring announcers that I like to see my own blood. I can't say that is really true, but I cannot say that it is false. I just know the harder the battle I am in, the more I am working to fulfill my purpose.

The truth is, I am fighting for people to show them what

they can become. I am fighting for people to *believe*. If I were fighting for anything but that, I would be angry with my opponents and I would want to hurt my opponents. It is quite the opposite. I pray for my opponent's safety. I pray that nobody will get hurt in that ring.

The dinner at the former president's home was supposed to be a casual dinner, not a business meeting. But all of a sudden, a contract was presented to me. Eric had struck a deal with another major company for me to be in photos and a commercial, and for this company to use my name, likeness, and image to help promote its product.

I never take these contracts for granted. They are a blessing, as each deal is not only an opportunity for me to earn more money for my family and for the businesses my wife and I love to create, but also for me to continue to hustle, to continue to try to be better than my competition.

I noticed right away that Jeng's signature is already on the contract. Each page was initialed by him, which meant it was a good deal for me and that I would have more money to share with the people on the streets.

Crack . . .

It's billiards night again. I make the next five balls in a row, and I feel like tonight is going to be a great night. I am in a place that is not as well lit as the home of the former president, adorned with big chandeliers. I do not see a hint of the beautiful marble that just two hours ago was everywhere. What I do see is life. I am back in my world, and it smells like the streets. It smells like the truth. It is a place where no one here can take advantage of me. People may try to hustle me on the tables because they think that is their game, and I am just a fighter. But this is what I know. I too know the game because I was not only born and raised on the streets, but also survived and thrived on the hustle.

CHAPTER TWELVE

My Life on Television

PEOPLE, MOSTLY REPORTERS or sports writers, ask me, "How does this nice guy, this warm and giving individual, also beat and pummel people in the ring?" Since this question comes up so much, perhaps I can answer it here.

I am not two different people. I have a life with my family and friends, and I have a job. At home, I'm not really focused on anything except enjoying my family. But when I'm at work, whether in the boxing ring or in the entertainment industry, I give it my all. Boxing is my profession, and I approach my work with an intensity that I wouldn't use in normal circumstances. My family and friends say that when I am with them my eyes are warm and friendly, but in the ring, against an opponent, my eyes are cold and aggressive, like an angry cat's.

In the ring, it is my job to do the best I can under those circumstances. That means winning and it means hitting people hard. It means focusing and concentrating every ounce of energy and strategy on that one individual—that one fight. It also means putting on a good show for my fans. I could not imagine disappointing my fans, because to me, that would be worse than losing. Before a fight, I always think of my fans, and this helps me prepare for the mental intensity I need.

As an art or science, boxing on the surface is not all that complicated. What can be complicated is planning for a particular fighter. I study my opponents over and over again, much of the time with videos of their past fights. I see their strengths and weaknesses, and then I strategize and plan for all of those elements. That is the difficult part of the *game*. If I had to maintain that level of discipline, concentration, and aggression in my daily life playing darts, billiards, or basketball, I would be very unhappy and exhausted. But I do apply this heightened focus and intensity into every fight and business venture, including in the television and entertainment industries.

In 2009, I was fortunate enough to get a starring role in a movie deal called *Wapakman*, and another starring role in a television show called *Show Me Da' Manny*. *Wapakman* was an action-comedy movie in the mold of another action movie, *Kung-Fu Hustle*. We filmed it in 2009 and I played the role of a Magno Manese, a plumber and a father with a lot of kids who possessed superpowers just like in *Kung-Fu Hustle*. It was really fun to do all the tricks and learning how to fly. *Show Me Da' Manny* was a romantic sitcom about an amateur boxing champ named Manny Santos—played by me—who runs a boxing gym called "Gym Santos" which he inherited from his parents.

I worked eight hours on one set just to go work another eight hours on the next set. These were two entirely different roles, too. So there I was filming *Wapakman*, and I was wearing this thick red outfit with a mask and learning how to fly with ropes attached to my body that are connected to a boom pole. I can tell you *that* role was a real workout. I gave that movie everything I had every single day—one hundred and ten percent.

After filming *Wapakman*, I would then be transported across town to the television station that was broadcasting my television show, *Show Me Da' Manny*.

This was an entirely different atmosphere. For one thing, I had a whole cast of actors with me, which was different from the movie set, which was centered around me and my character. I really had fun on both sets, but *Show Me Da' Manny* was one of those life experiences that just did not feel like work. The cast and I would spend most of the time on- and off-camera laughing and having fun. I can honestly say that this was one of the most fun experiences and one of the highlights of my life. The show got great ratings, but the best part was that I made lifetime friends with whom I will have special bonds forever.

I even flew some of the cast in for the Cotto fight and let them experience everything firsthand. I wanted to show them the time of their lives.

It is experiences like these that really make you smile and thank God every day and every night for your blessings. I hope my children will learn this, and I hope I will be a good father who can teach them how important each experience is in your life and that it doesn't have to be the ones that might at first seem to be the most important.

Sometimes, it can be the experiences that are not every-day occurrences or things that might never happen again in your life.

CHAPTER THIRTEEN

Training a Philippine Warrior

MUCH ATTENTION HAS been given by the media recently to the use of performance-enhancing drugs by athletes in many sports. From cycling, to football, to baseball, it seems no sport is immune, including boxing. I have never been concerned about someone randomly checking my blood or urine for these drugs because I have never used anabolic steroids and, in fact, I don't even know what they look like. I have always volunteered to have my urine tested at any time, all the way up to the moment I am walking into the ring. But then, it was brought to my attention that synthetic growth hormone cannot be tested for in our urine. It is only detected in blood tests.

In my opinion, taking blood from a person weakens them, which is not something any fighter can afford just before a fight. Because of this, I have had some concerns about the amount of blood that can be taken from me for testing too close to a fight. Some have criticized my stance on this issue, but my objection to the testing wasn't ever about the testing itself—it was always about the timing of the testing. I do not want to be in a weakened state when I enter the ring against any fighter. It isn't safe for me, nor does it honor the hard work and preparation I undertake before a fight.

I view using steroids, synthetic growth hormone, or any other illegal or banned substance as cheating—plain and simple. I would never cheat this sport that I love. I would never cheat the legacies of the great champions I have been blessed to challenge. I would never do anything to cheat such great champions as Miguel Cotto, Ricky Hatton, and all of the Mexican Warriors that I have been blessed to go into the ring and do battle with. I believe all of these men have great honor for boxing, for their country, and for themselves. They are heroes to me. These are people I have great respect and admiration for.

As boxers, we risk our lives every time we enter the ring. We risk our health and our livelihood. This is a very dangerous sport, so I take my training very seriously. I train thirty rounds a day, every day, to be in the best shape during a fight so that I can give the fans the best show I possibly can. I eat very healthily almost all of the time—lots of chicken, fish, and rice.

In order to make the heavier weight classes I have to eat more than I have ever eaten in my life—eating bigger meals five times a day. I eat foods that build muscle. I work out hard. I stay very focused and disciplined towards my goal. I focus on success.

God has blessed me with my abilities, and I give all the glory to Him. I try and let God use me as an example of what someone can be if they never give up, and if they work hard and believe in themselves. I believe there are three things in life you need in order to be successful, things that have nothing to do with where you live or how much money is in your wallet. Perhaps you sleep on a bed made out of cardboard. Or maybe you live in a mansion. It doesn't matter what your circumstances are. The three things you need to instill in your life are goals, a system to reach your goals, and the discipline to maintain your system until you reach your goals. I call these three steps the "Power Three." They might sound simple and obvious, but many people often overlook these important principles, or find them too difficult to maintain. I promise that anyone can do them, and achieve success regardless of who you are or what you want to acheive.

At fifteen, I wanted to be the lightweight champion of the world, but at that time it just wasn't practical or feasible. I had never fought a professional fight in my life, plus I did not have the weight on my body to fight at that weight class. I also didn't have the skill or the people around me to help me make it there. But what I did have was a goal.

Next, I asked myself, "What will it take me to get there?" The reality of the situation is that I was no where close to my goal. I realized that the farther you are away from reaching your ultimate goal, the more you need intermediate goals. So the answer became very clear to me. I needed to set smaller goals as guideposts and touchstones on my way to the ultimate victory. It may take you a bit longer to get to your ultimate goal, but that's when discipline is critical. The journey will be worth it as you achieve many small victories along the way. I started to think of everything it would take for me to achieve the smaller goals, and, among other things, this included designing a game plan. When I started realizing everything it would take to become the lightweight champion, I understood that this was going to take a lot of work, a lot of prayer, and a lot of discipline.

My first intermediate goal in becoming the lightweight champion of the world was really just to find somewhere to learn how to box and to find someone very skilled who could teach me. Until then, I would make the best of everything I had around me. My Uncle Sardo, who lived in General Santos City—the one who built a gym in his house—was more than enough of a teacher for me. I had that completely covered.

Then I needed food and sustenance. Without food to fuel my training, I would never achieve my goal. While most may take this for granted, you have to remember that early in my boxing career, I was struggling to survive on a day-to-day basis. So with very little resource, I aimed to eat the cheapest and the healthiest food available to me—fish and rice. That's what I would eat the most of and, really, I didn't want anything else. Based on all my years of hustling on the streets, I knew how many hours I would need to work to make enough money so I could eat each day.

I already had a home I could sleep in every night, even though it wasn't anything special. In fact, most people would have probably looked at my small little place where I lived and just given up right there. I was just thankful that I had a roof over my head, as well as fish and rice to eat every day, and clean drinking water to drink every day. Fortunately, I didn't need much to be happy in those early days, and these modest accommodations were all I needed to be better the next day.

That was my first goal, my first system, and my first act of discipline. I would simply be better the next day than I was the day before.

My Early Training

When I started training with Uncle Sardo, I couldn't run five miles without getting tired. I couldn't throw jabs or punches, and I couldn't bob or weave. I couldn't even stand in front of you and protect myself as I hit you. So we had to start with conditioning and basic training.

Running was best conditioning exercise. When I first started running, I could only go about two or three miles at a time. But as I continued to train, I could run four or five miles rather quickly and with minimal effort.

After my workout, I would go to my uncle's home, put on my gloves, and start hitting the bag. I would work with my uncle to throw jabs, hooks, crosses, body punches, and straight lead punches. You name it, we worked on it.

Uncle Sardo would hold mitts for me and let me hit moving targets. Then, he would try and hit me back with the mitts so I would have to duck and move to avoid his hard punches. He worked to teach me to keep my hands up and move my head from side to side. Then he would work with me on my stance and my balance. We covered all the basics, and did everything we could do to build a better boxer inside that house.

Each and every day, I went back to see my uncle, and every day, we got better together. My uncle would watch other fighters on television and then he would teach me to do what they did. I became a better boxer, and he became a better teacher. It was fun to be learning together.

Conditioning Today

Today, my training regimen is not much different than it was back in 1989. Now, I just have more people around me who are more educated on training elite athletes. My training regimen for a fight usually takes place in Los Angeles, where I love to run every morning. I do try to change up my routine every day so that I won't get bored. The key is always to challenge myself and to stay disciplined. There are mornings where I'll run four miles in beautiful, tree-lined Griffith Park in Los Angeles, or I'll run the track near my house. Fans might even spot me at a local high school where I do sprints on the football field or on their track. Other days, I'll jog all the way to the top of the Griffith Park Observatory, which is a steep, uphill run to the place where James Dean filmed his classic movie, *Rebel Without a Cause.*

After my run, I stretch. These are not the typical touch your toes stretch. These stretching exercises that my trainers have me work on are intense and sometimes painful.

The next stop is some serious, gut-burning sit-ups or crunches that help strengthen my core. Another way I develop my core during training is to sit on the ground with my legs out in front of me, bent just slightly. Someone on the side of me will throw me a medicine ball that might weigh ten pounds. I will turn to the side and catch the ball. Then I twist my body from my waist up and bring my body back to where I can throw the ball back to the guy. Try this only a few times when starting your training regimen and I promise you will feel it the next day!

I attend to my core strength because everything in boxing is based from your core: lower back strength, toned sides, strong abdominal muscles, and flexible, strong hips. When your core is tight and strong, your legs are able to pull from this base. If you just develop strong legs then you will tire quickly. The key is to develop the middle of your body first and then the upper body, including shoulders and arms, plus your upper back. Your mind also feeds off the strength of your core because if you're less tired, you can focus better.

When I'm in the ring, I get stronger as the match continues into the rounds. I'll have as much energy at the end of the fight as at the beginning. This allows my mind to work better, which keeps me smarter in the ring. In my humble opinion, it makes me smarter than my opponent. Can you imagine what happens to your thought process when you're dead tired and someone is hitting you in the head? It's definitely not a good feeling. I have developed my body from the core so that my body can function efficiently and pull all of the energy from the strongest parts.

Today, I still rely on the Power Three to achieve my goals.

CHAPTER FOURTEEN

Packing Punches, Food Baskets, and Medical Kits

MANY PEOPLE SAY when I fight, the entire country stops and watches—literally. People scurry to find television sets and sit down with friends or family to watch. The police in Manila say that the crime rate drops during my fights, which means that even the criminals stop their dirty work for at least an hour or so. The police wish I would fight more often. I'm proud that my accomplishments don't end in the ring.

From a reporter's notebook

Manny Pacquiao not only helps give back to his home country, he understands that people need help and support throughout the world. In America, Manny has contributed to planting trees for the fight against global warming and has helped numerous charities raise money. The best thing about Manny "Pacman" Pacquiao is that he personally participates in everything he supports. He is not just

a face who will show up to an event. He will par-
ticipate with the people and becomes a part of the
moment.

I remember vividly when Typhoon Ondoy hit Manila while I was training for the Miguel Cotto fight. Although I wasn't able to physically help with the disaster relief, I did what I could by helping The Manny Pacquiao Foundation raise money to help the victims. The first day I could break away and leave training camp, I returned to Manila. I had to be with my people. But I was not the only Pacquiao who helped. Even Team Pacquiao in Los Angeles organized fundraisers and sent shipments of relief supplies. Such collective relief effort by the people around me was very touching because it showed me that my closest friends not only supported me but also shared my vision and love for my people.

● ● ● ● ● ●

"Manny Pacquiao Helps Typhoon Vic-
tims." *This headline ran in an online story in Oc-
tober 2009. The article reports that after the
devastating typhoon that struck the Philippines,
Manny, during his day off from training, traveled
to Metro Manila and Rizal to show his support for*

the ongoing relief operation. He helped pack the re-lief goods and handed them to the typhoon victims himself, and he donated one million pesos to aid the unfortunate victims of this natural disaster. This contribution was made to Oplan Ondoy, one of the many relief organizations Manny supports through his Manny Pacquiao Foundation project to help al-leviate the sad condition of the victims in the after-math of the worst typhoon ever experienced in Manila and Luzon.

This one-week campaign, which was immedi-ately launched after typhoon Ondoy hit, generated an overwhelming number of bags of used clothing, sacks of rice, assorted boxes of canned and packed goods and milk powder, as well as other necessities.

● ● ● ● ● ●

MARCH 7, 2009 was a very special day for me. I was asked by the Mayor of Los Angeles, Antonio Villaraigosa, to help him promote a green-earth movement to fight global warm-ing. Growing up in the green mountains of Tango, I have a special appreciation for Mother Nature, and preserving Mother Earth is another one of my passions. Therefore, I was more than happy to help. As a bonus, they were having this event in Filipino Town, so it was very close to where I lived in Los Angeles and would not interrupt my training schedule for the upcoming Ricky Hatton fight.

I showed up on March 7 to enjoy the scenes in Filipino Town. To my surprise, I found the media and a crowd people gathered there to witness me planting a tree with Mayor Villaraigosa. The mayor was extremely gracious when receiving me and said, "This is a day of service and Manny Pacquiao is a great champion, a great human being, an environmentalist, a man who understands that fame and celebrity come with a responsibility to the community. He's a true champion. We recognize he's a busy man and for the fact that he would take time out to participate in this tree planting, which is commemorative of the restoration of a community, is a real honor." Although Mayor Villaraigosa admitted that he had rooted for Oscar De La Hoya in our "Dream Match" fight, he then went on to say that I was a pound-for-pound champion outside the ring as well as inside the ring, and presented me a large, framed certificate of appreciation. His words and gesture really touched my heart and made me feel welcomed in my second home, Los Angeles. All I could do at that moment was smile and say, "Thank you very much, Mr. Mayor, for inviting me here to be part of this program to plant one million trees in Los Angeles. I'm very proud to be part of this program."

The very next weekend, and less than six weeks out from my fight with Ricky Hatton, I was asked to go to Orange

County, California to attend a fundraiser for a safety-aware-
ness organization called the "Breathe Again Foundation,"
founded by a friend. The organization raises awareness to
prevent child drowning. I love children. So even though I
was only six weeks out from my fight with Ricky Hatton, I
was delighted to attend this organization's first fundraiser,
which was a charity poker tournament. It turns out that I was
the main draw—a chance to play poker against Manny Pacquiao. I had a great time. I took fifth place after being
knocked out by Gary Randal, the owner of MaxBoxing.com.
It was a great evening, and Bruce Buffer, the voice of the *Oc-
tagon*, was there to call the tournament.

From the founder of Breathe Again Foundation

> *I cannot begin to tell you the difference Manny made
> to our event and our lives for taking the time out
> of his life to help ours. When people around our
> area heard they had the ability to take out the
> champ in a game of poker, our attendance tripled.
> People started donating more and companies
> wanted to get involved.*
>
> *The night before the event, I was told by a mem-
> ber of Team Pacquiao Los Angeles that Manny was
> inclined not to attend the event because he had to
> spar the next day and would be too exhausted. I*

immediately drove to Los Angeles that night and ask Manny to reconsider. I then told him I would have a limousine pick him up so he did not have to drive. Manny just looked at me and said, "How much will that limousine cost you?" I told him it would be about a thousand dollars. I told him that it was very important to my family and our charity. Manny then looked to one of his right-hand members of Team Pacquaio L.A., Edward Lura, and said. "Tomorrow, we go to Tim's charity." He then looked me in the eye and said, "Tim, you do not pay for a limousine. You keep that money for your event. I will drive myself."

But he didn't drive. He truly did not want to drive while training for his fight. The next night he arrived in a stretch Hummer limousine with thirty people. He used his own money to provide for transportation and brought his whole team with him for an incredible event. Manny did not just attend our event, he actively participated in it, playing poker, billiards, and darts. He took photos with everyone, signed autographs, and was one of the last people to leave.

Needless to say, in my eyes, Manny Pacquiao is a real hero.

I believe that we are given things in life as a gift to give to others. Just because you have money does not mean that you are supposed to keep and enjoy that money for yourself. We are given certain responsibilities because we can handle them, and it is our duty to be responsible with our blessings. I often carry thousands of pesos in my pockets when strolling through the streets in the Philippines. Knowing the money is there, impoverished children would gather around me and reach in my pockets to grab the money. They knew I would have the money and this money would feed them that day. I gladly let them reach because it's a sign of my love, and I believe anytime you can show love then there is no harm. So I let them reach for now, but I realize that love alone cannot be the long term solution. It has to be education.

I understand the importance of education, as I, too, suffered as I didn't receive the education that I wanted so I could become a priest. It wasn't until later in life that I was able to finish high school by passing my GED and started college courses. But by then, it was too late for me to pursue my dream. Because of my educational experience or lack thereof, I founded a scholarship program that provides financial grants to those ensnared by poverty. Over one thousand students have benefited from this scholarship program, and the number continues to grow.

But education is not the only area of need in the

Philippines. There is so much to do. Homelessness, hunger, and medical care to name just a few. One of the most gratifying moments in my life was when my foundation, "The Manny 'Pacman' Foundation Inc.," formed a medical mission team with over thirty doctors, nurses, and other support staff. The team has traveled throughout the Philippines to remote cities and regions to provide medical care to the poor. On one of these missions, over 6,000 people showed up, and we did not leave until everyone was cared for.

After the Oscar De La Hoya fight, I vowed to donate one million Philippine pesos to the hospital in General Santos City for each of my fights. Earlier this year, I learned that my donation helped a patient who needed a kidney transplant, and now that man is healthy and able to live a normal life. When I was preparing for my political campaign, that man came to my home and asked if he could campaign with me so that he could tell everyone what I had done for him. I sat him down and thanked him, but then told him that I could not accept his generous support because my philanthropic work was separate and apart from my political career. I do not want my charity work be viewed as a political ploy or photo opportunity because it isn't. I told the man that seeing him alive and healthy in my living room was gift enough.

It is stories like these that motivate me to work hard outside the ring as I do inside the ring. Today, the Manny "Pacman" Pacquiao Foundation, Inc. employs over two hundred caring people. Each of these people, who labor with me to care for the poor, the needy, and the down-trodden has my most sincere gratitude and respect. I couldn't do it without them.

From Lennox Lewis, former World Heavyweight Champion and boxing commentator for HBO, in a *TIME* magazine article :

Pound for pound, Manny is the best boxer in the world, but even more important than holding that distinction, Manny has connected with the people of his home country, the Philippines, to the point where he is almost like a god.

The people have rallied behind him and feel like they're a part of him because they can see his talent, his dedication, his grace, and his class. The grip he holds over the Philippines is similar to Nelson Mandela's influence in South Africa. I can surely see Manny becoming the President of the Philippines one day.

In fact, he already ran for Congress in the Philippines {once} but lost, in part because voters thought he could do more for the country as an in-spirational champion boxer. [Editor: Manny has been elected to Congress since Lennox wrote this.] *I agree with the Filipino people.*

Manny, 30, already has a true global reach, and his influence will only expand as he gets better. Manny is from the Muhammad Ali school; he's a boxer, a puncher, and a mover. He doesn't stand there and take shots. He throws that wicked jab and is quick to dodge trouble.

Boxing needs a guy like Manny. He just loves the sport and knows he's carrying the hopes of his country into the ring.

CHAPTER FIFTEEN

The Great Race for Congress

TO MOST PEOPLE, I am a philanthropic boxing champion. But being a boxing champion and a philanthropist isn't enough for me because there are too many people who need help. These same young men and women are struggling each night to find their supper while keeping their dreams alive. These are boys and girls who years ago could have been my twins. They are thin, hungry, but hopeful. There was no way I could help every single one of them in my position as a boxer. I knew there had to be a better way to reach and work for *all* my people.

Over the years, friends and supporters suggested that someday I run for political office and affect sweeping and lasting change for my countrymen. I knew that "someday" must come sooner rather than later. For my people, we don't have the luxury of time. Their tomorrow needs action right today, and my running for political office is the only solution for me to help them.

My first venture into politics was in 2007. I ran for a seat in the Philippines' House of Representatives on a platform that was universally simple—education, health-care and economy. Specifically, I proposed free education and healthcare to the poor. I also proposed giving small boats to fishermen and financially supporting small neighborhood businesses. While my platform was simple, politics wasn't. I was solidly defeated by a powerful scion of the Philippines—a local businesswoman who came from a wealthy family. My opponent was a woman named Darlene Magnolia Antonino-Custodio, a representative of the first district of South Cotabato and General Santos City. She was a seasoned opponent with politics in her blood. Darlene came from the prominent Antonino Clan of South Cotabato, where her father and mother, Aldelbert and Luwalhati R. Antonino, both served as mayor and in the House of Representatives for General Santos City and South Cotabato. She was also the granddaughter of Senators Guadencio and Magnolia Antonio, plus she was married to Benjamin Custodio, a prominent businessman.

Even my closest advisors warned me that I would probably lose to her. Jeng and others advised me that the goodwill that I earned from professional boxing was no match against someone from a formidable and respected political family. It hurt me when I was defeated because I don't like to lose at anything. But I blamed myself because I didn't really know how to campaign. My campaign was rushed and disorganized. I decided to run for office in January 2007, I trained and fought Solis in April 2007, and the election was in May 2007. With only a few weeks of campaigning, I didn't really have much of a chance. Perhaps I was overly optimistic or perhaps I gave too much weight to my popularity and goodwill, but one thing was for sure, I was not about to give up. My passion and dream to help my fellow country still burned within my heart. The 2007 election only fueled that passion. The election results not only remind me that I needed to trust those close to me but also taught me that I needed to earn the trust of my people for them to elect me to office.

Indeed, did I decide to wave the white flag? I hope you know me better by now. I knew that my next run would be an even bigger race. And I knew I had to run a far more sophisticated and organized campaign.

For my second run at the office, I announced my candidacy in November 2009. My campaign headquarters was a two-room office in General Santos City. I was our country's first athlete to ever run for such a high office. But why not represent the people when I was clearly still one of them? Who could be better than a local boy who knew their struggles?

"I don't know of any major boxer who is also a politician," said my promoter Bob Arum, who was one of the first to join me on the campaign trail. He was quick to wave "Manny for Congress" posters and distribute flyers to our workers, who combed the neighborhoods spreading the word. We asked the people if they want to be represented by someone from a rich family who had never faced the struggles of daily life or if they wanted someone who had lived it until he could find a better way.

I wanted to show my countrymen and women how people should be treated and that they shouldn't stand for the corruption of their government taking advantage of them and using their tax dollars for the luxuries of the rich. I knew our government was, for the most part, corrupt and that most of the politicians who had been voted into office were taking advantage of our people.

After an election, most of these politicos just focused on how they were going to get their campaign money back and how to line their pockets with even more money. It was never about how they would serve the people in order for them to lead better lives.

I explained to my people that I would use the money for the public good, including building necessary facilities such as hospitals, schools, and recreational centers. I even promised that I would build boxing gyms throughout the province so children could live the dream while becoming stronger and healthier citizens.

When I was finished talking to my people, I asked if they liked what they heard. I would hear a strong *yes*, and then I would ask them if they would vote for me. Again, I would hear a strong *yes*.

Then I would tell them, "That is not enough. There are many people who are not here right now. They can't hear what I will do for them and how they are being taken advantage of by the government that's in place now." I needed these people to go back to their homes, back to their neighborhoods, and back to their jobs to tell everyone what they had heard from me. I told everyone I needed their help, just as they needed mine. I reminded them if they truly wanted me to win then I needed them to go and spread the word and get more people to vote for me.

I didn't just campaign from a platform—I went out to the people. I walked with them, spoke to them, listened to them. I was with parents, business owners, workers, farmers and the every day person. I did this for twelve hours a day and at least six days a week.

Jinkee did the same thing, except she would go to different areas of the province so we could cover more ground. As always, she was truly a blessing for me during this entire campaign. Jinkee and her strong family went out in five or six cars, which included her mom, dad, sisters, brothers, and her closest friends. They would go out into the heart of the cities and speak on my behalf, pass out fliers, shake hands, and tell people that they were being treated unfairly, but that change was in the air.

I think what most of the world doesn't realize is that

many of my countrymen and women aren't even aware of the possibilities for a better life. It's tragic that they don't realize that the money that is supposed to be used for their needs is either wasted or stolen from them. I wanted to tell them that they didn't need to work so hard for so little while going hungry every single day. Their family members didn't have to remain sick, or, sadly, die, because they couldn't afford healthcare.

There are tens of thousands of people in my country who don't even know that free healthcare is a possibility. Jinkee, her family, and her friends were also spreading that message, and I'm forever in their debt because I couldn't campaign alone. The best way for me to pay them back was to show them one day how much better people's lives have become in the province that was Jinkee's childhood home. I knew we could bring those necessary messages to the masses.

Campaigning wasn't easy. It occurred to me that suddenly I wasn't the known champion, but the underdog again. In fact, it reminded me of the feelings I had in 2008 before my fight with Oscar De La Hoya. But with that feeling of having to prove something came the great will to see a victory.

As in boxing, I had to size up my opponent for my second run for congress. He was a U.S.-educated, wealthy businessman, Roy Chiongblan—a man from a very rich family, who was also twice my age. He also had political clout on his side because for over four decades his family had never been defeated in local politics. This would be a true "David and Goliath" story. I knew that I had to keep my focus tight and so I campaigned on the age-old issues of poverty and corruption.

"I know what poverty is," I told a group of villagers who had gathered in Malandag during one of my campaign rallies. "I come from a poor family. I was once you, and I know I could be back there again. And I want to change our country for our children so they don't have to go to bed hungry."

It was a simple but powerful message. The faces in front of me showed me that they were hearing the words and taking them to heart.

Election day was one of the most exciting, dangerous, and thrilling days of my entire life. When I woke up I noticed that a storm was rolling in, and sure enough, within hours the skies were the darkest of grays, the winds were very powerful, and it started to pour rain. Immediately, I thought of all the people that were going to go out and vote and how the voting in the Philippines is extremely frustrating because the people could not easily vote. Most had to stand in long lines for hours just to cast their votes. But for this election, there was an important change in that the country had finally instituted the first fully-automated voting machines.

On election day, I woke up very early and could not wait to go to my province and cast my vote. I got up, showered, and got dressed, wondering if this was the day that would change my life forever and if this was the day that would hopefully change the lives of the people in Sanangani forever.

Hopping into my waiting blacked-out and bomb-proofed Hummer, I followed my police escort to the election polls, where I was the 110th person to cast my vote in the early morning hours. It did my heart good to see that the lines had already began forming and that everyone was staying positive, holding their umbrellas, and accepting the brisk wind and rain in their faces as something that was part of the struggle of having the freedom to vote and the freedom to change.

After voting, I was then escorted back to my home in General Santos, where I joined Jinkee for what would be one of the longest days of my life. We pretended to relax with my family and friends, but I kept checking the clock. It was still early and the elections would not end until seven o'clock that evening. There was nothing else I could do to campaign and what I needed to do now was work with my team to manage the polls as best we could to make sure that nobody would tamper with the results. My wish was simple in that I just wanted a fair vote and not one that was swayed by corrupt businessmen looking to line their own pockets.

Most of the day was spent watching the polling results and staying on the phone with my campaign staff in order to pinpoint the mood of my countrymen. These were people who often earned less than two US dollars a day and who might not even earn that on election day if they couldn't get their work done while voting. Yet, that vote meant a better future for them, so most were willing to forgo the little food they could afford that day for a bigger dream.

By late afternoon, I knew that the results were about 80 percent in my favor—which was an amazing landslide—but it wasn't official as of yet, so my emotions were still a bit ragged. Barely allowing this good news to sink in, I heard the laughter and excitement from my campaign staffers who were watching the results come in.

Suddenly, it seemed as if change could be possible. I heard that it would be impossible to replace a Chiongbian, but I always figured that the impossible could be possible if you tried hard enough.

That night, the newscasters suggested that it was my work with the people—and not my charitable contribution to the people that gave me the victory. I was known for walking the streets after my fights and handing out food and money to my fellow Filipinos—men, women and children, and investing in schools and medical clinics in a quiet way without any fanfare.

Only the results.

It did my heart good to see the coconut farmers, tuna fishermen, and laborers make their way to the polls. Bribery was rampant, which was common during an election in the Philippines. Yes, the country spent $7.2 billion pesos ($15.5 million U.S.) on these voting machines, but it was easy to manipulate the Smartcards within them. There was word that some were offering to pay off poor workers in order to vote for a certain candidate. For $21.50 (US), they were asked to "sell" their votes. This kind of money could provide food for over a week for a family, so it must have been very tempting. In some areas, the new voting machines were disabled when they thought the vote would be overwhelmingly in my favor.

These small moments were heartbreaking for me. The Malandag Central Elementary School in the municipality of Malungon had 48,270 registered voters who mostly waited in long lines outside during a torrential rainstorm in order to mostly vote for me in a tiny classroom that had two voting machines.

It was *Pacman all the way* for them.

"There is a feeling that Pacquiao is one of us, one of the people, so we want to choose the right candidate to help us, and that's Manny," said Cynthia Leandres, a healthcare worker. She carried an umbrella with the logo "Totoong ("Truly") Manny Pacquiao."

In another area that favored Chiongbian, called Alabel,

41,279 registered voters felt the pressure because most of them worked at Chiongbian-owned banana and coconut plantations. Yet there were whispers all around of people saying, "We voted for our Pacman."

"I've heard reports of (vote-buying) here, yes," said Liberal Party poll watcher, Eugenia Manacio of Alabel. Her voting site experienced brownouts and power failures in what was a particularly friendly area for me. When the area went black from a power failure, she connected her voting machine to a motorcycle battery. Suddenly, she was back in business.

Meanwhile, the sun went down, and at 7:00 PM, I left my home and my family to go man the post at what was secretly known as the "Pentagon." This was a secret headquarters of sorts where we did a lot of our political strategizing and maneuvering. This was also the home of my right-hand man who helped with every detail of my election from the very beginning, and is one of the main reasons I can have the final chapter of my book dedicated to me winning the race. His name is (Mayor) Tani Pepito and he was partnered with my good friend and also my right-hand man for this campaign, Zaldy Du. The home is modest, but very nice, and Mayor Pepito completely opened it up to my family and all of my workers.

Another member of the team that really helped me to win is Michael Koncz. Mike is my head of staff in the U.S. and an advisor to me. Mike had to take on an entirely new role during my political campaign, which was to oversee the budget and help me to manage where the money was going. There were many times that the budget in some areas went above and beyond what we had originally anticipated, but somehow Mike always found a way to just get it done. I think my wife put it best when she told Mike, "You know, Mike, the problem you have with Manny is that you always come through for him and you never let him down. That is the reason he keeps asking you to do more and more. He trusts you will never let him down."

We set up our base in the back of Mayor Pepito's home, which was a two room maid's quarters equipped with its own bathroom. We brought in 15 computers, landlines, printers, walkie-talkies, phones, radios, tables for food, and huge chalkboards and dry-erase boards to lay out our game plan and to manage the entire campaign—all from this 900-square-foot quarters of a home that was tucked away behind a fence in General Santo City.

That night, I hopped in my black Hummer and was followed by my escort, except this time it was a little bit different. Vehicles that contained writers from *Time* magazine, CNN, and other news organizations, along with Mike Marely, and Bob Arum, joined us. When we first got to the location, I showed everyone around and explained how we used this place to continually monitor the campaign. Monitoring meant waiting, and I was anxious.

At approximately 9:45 PM, a call that came through on one of our small military style black hand-held radios.

"Manny," someone stated, "the poll watchers have the first numbers of the votes." My heart must have stopped just for the briefest of seconds, as everything we had worked for over the past year was now finished.

Pacquiao, 374 / Chiongbian, 110

Pacquiao, 639 / Chiongbian, 228

Pacquiao, 888 / Chiongbian, 605

Pacquiao, 594 / Chiongbian, 85

My smile was huge because I then got a phone call confirming that the first votes had come in and in all of the cities they were showing I was leading the race. It was turning into a landslide—this time in my favor.

This was one of the most incredible nights of my life— much different than boxing, and much different than winning a title. It was like all my life I had been giving to my country, and my country just gave everything back to me. They said, "Manny, we love you, and we trust you. Please make our lives better."

Bob was there by my side all night. He made the trip all the way from the United States, and he played a key role in my victory. I believe when the people of the province saw Bob Arum with me they saw that I was able to bring in powerful people from other parts of the world, and that these powerful people would care about making their lives better just as I would.

By 10:30 PM that night, a local reporter called Roy Chiongbian's nephew and asked him to concede.

Bob would actually up the ante. He decided to offer my opponent ringside seats and a suite to my next fight . . . if he conceded. Bob just needed a messenger to deliver the offer. So, he approached reporter Mike Marley and stated, "If you were a real reporter, you would not be here getting the easy information from Manny at his headquarters."

Mike's jaw dropped.

"A real reporter would go to the losing candidate's home and find out what is going on there," Bob teased him.

Mike Marely, who is the most heralded writer for Pacman, and who has been in the boxing industry since the heady days of Howard Cosell and Muhammad Ali, didn't blink at going through enemy lines.

This was very brave of him, because the previous week there had been bomb threats swirling around different political candidates, and on election night there was an "anything could happen" danger in the air.

There is also a known rule in the Philippines that you don't want to be on the streets the night of an election, especially if you are a member of the opposition. You could easily get kidnapped—or worse.

Mike immediately took the challenge and wanted the opportunity to go ask Chiongbian if he felt he was losing, and if so, what did this mean to him and his family. He would naturally remind him that this would be their family's first defeat in over forty years and his first defeat ever. It was obvious that Mike's visit wouldn't be an easy one.

Bob then told Mike that he could spice it up and bit and tell Chiongbian that if he would concede the race to me right then, Bob would personally give him two ringside seats, and a suite to boot. Bob even wrote that promise on a piece of paper and handed it to Mike with Bob's signature on the bottom to make it official.

Hopping into a van with one of my security men, along with reporters from *Time* magazine and CNN, Mike drove through enemy territory and made it all the way to Chiongbian's headquarters, which was a home he lived in part-time in the province of Sarangani.

He was shocked when he found that the premises were pitch black. There wasn't one light shining through the house and there was no activity going on inside the gates.

Mike did find a lone bodyguard of Chiongbian's and was told that the whole Chiongbian party had gone to sleep as soon as the numbers started going in my direction.

There was definitely no celebration happening at that residence.

Somehow, Mike made it back to our headquarters in one piece and that fact alone caused another celebration. It was obvious that Chiongbian had given up and was somehow accepting his fate and sleeping through what was probably one of the worst nights of his life.

Of course, there were still two ringside seats available to him for one my upcoming fights. On this crucial night, Marley did not have the ability to offer them to Chiongbian, but a promise is a promise.

The results continued to pour in and they were resoundingly in my favor. I told my staff to call it a night at 2 AM, and figured that we would find out our fate in the morning.

As the sun rose the next day, the people seemed to know that a new era had also dawned.

"I don't know how to explain how happy I am," said Zaldy Du the next morning. Zaldy is a local businessman and trader who offered me his home as one of my campaign centers. "I am accepting no money for this. No payment for the power. I'm doing it because I'm the number one boxing fan of Manny Pacquiao," he said.

It was a touching moment for me.

In the early morning hours, I was named the winner. It was May 10, 2010 when I won a seat in my country's Congress by a landside.

The headlines the next day were surreal, but gratifying:

Manny Pacquiao Finally Rests After "Landslide" Victory

In this article, Ronnie Nathanielsz (http://www.box-ingscene.com), wrote: "Pound-for-pound king Manny Pacquiao is resting in his home in General Santos City after scoring a stunning victory over Roy Chiongbian in the battle for the lone congressional seat in Sarangani province. There were many who didn't believe Pacquiao could overcome the well-entrenched Chiongbian clan and a solid political organization that backed him up but like the many spectacular victories in the boxing ring against such hugely favored fighters like Oscar De La Hoya, Ricky Hatton and earlier in his career Marco Antonio Barrera, Pacquiao silenced the non-believers with what amounts to a landslide victory."

Manny Pacquiao's Latest Win— in Philippine Election

"It was a fight even Manny Pacquiao's closest advisers warned he would lose. His opponent hailed from a formidable political family. And the last time the Filipino boxing sensation ran for public office, he lost badly. But on Monday, May 10, Pacquiao won a seat in his country's Congress—and won it by a landslide. 'A congressman!' he says with a grin, clearly still grappling with the concept, as he exchanges hugs and handshakes with staff at 'the Pentagon,' the code name for his two-room campaign headquarters in General Santos City. 'It's the first time in history.' And what a concept—not just for a tyro congressman from Sarangani, a remote province in the southern Philippines, but for the sport that brought this local boy fame and riches. 'I don't know of any major boxer who has also been a politician,' says his promoter Bob Arum, 78, who joined Pacquiao on his campaign trail.

"The last time Pacquiao was considered the underdog was in 2008 when he fought his hero Oscar De La Hoya. Then, as now, he demolished his opponent. U.S.-educated businessman Roy Chiongbian was twice his age and had never run for office, but his family had dominated local politics for three decades. Like almost every other candidate during this election, Pacquiao campaigned on the familiar issues of poverty and corruption. 'I know what poverty is,' he told villagers in Malandag during his last rally. 'I come from a poor family.'

"This simple message resonated. Pacquiao won big not just in Kiamba, where he spent part of his youth, but in other areas of Sarangani previously considered Chiongbian strongholds. Arum, who once represented Muhammad Ali, was rhapsodic—and not just because promoting 'Boxing Congressman' will do wonders for those pay-per-view figures. 'Ali was a wonderful person, but it was more about Ali,' says Arum. 'This kid spent a fortune running for office.

And he did it not to aggrandize himself but because he really believes he can make a difference.'" (Andrew Marshall, General Santos City, (http://www.time.comwww.time.com)

Pacquiao Goes to Congress was the headline in *The Manila Times*. In this piece, Ed C. Tolentino wrote: "Contrary to what some quarters believe, the transition from ring tactician to politician doesn't figure to be that difficult for Pacquiao. Bluntly speaking, work in Congress does not equate to brain surgery. Pacquiao can simply surround himself with a battery of good lawyers and half the work is done."

"A congressman," I kept repeating, with a grin spreading wide across my face. It was almost as if I couldn't believe it myself. This exhilarating win was accompanied by more exchanges of hugs and more flesh pressing than I had ever experienced as a boxer.

The truth was, I had demolished my opponent and it felt great. I was told that my landslide wasn't just in Kiamba, where I grew up, but in various other areas of Sarangani, which were always known as territories for my opponent and his family.

Almost immediately, Bob Arum began to call me the "Boxing Congressman."

"Manny, this will do wonders for our pay-per-view figures," he joked with me.

Some asked if politics was just a part of my retirement plan. After all, I was thirty-one years old when I won my congressional seat and my mother had already been vocal about me retiring while I was still strong and healthy. I heard detractors taunt me and say that several Filipino sports stars, including our best-known basketball players, had traded the fame of sports for the fame of public office with its wealth and influence. My reason for running had nothing to do with obvious gains.

I know it sounds very basic, but I just want to help my people. Isn't that enough? Isn't that what public work is supposed to be about when stripped to its core? I knew that my people had given me so much because without them I wouldn't be a world-famous boxer. Now, it was my turn to give back to them.

"Without your support, there would be no Manny Pacquiao," I told villagers at another rally, and those words were honest and true.

I took a hit for spending so much on my election. But the truth was, I needed to win in order to work on the important issues. If life in the ring taught me one thing, it's that you do what you need to do in order to be the last man standing. Now, I prefer to think of it as Chiongbian folding. I hit him with a knockout punch and he never stood up again.

By the way, I financed my own campaign because of my

Tango Elementary School where Manny and Bobby attended as children.

The Boxing Brothers at the gym.

Taking on Freddie Roach.

Manny and Bobby: brothers, friends and training partners—building off one another their whole lives.

Ceremonial first pitch
at LA Angels game.

BELOW: Running the
track with his dog,
Pacman, in Las Vegas.

BOTTOM: Manny getting
a workout before the Clottey
fight in Los Angeles.

Manny and Jinkee inside their Los Angeles home.

Mama D gets a necklace at her birthday party in 2010.

Happy family!

Manny and Jinkee out for an evening.

LA producer Amy Almerol with Manny at the Fire Power press conference.

LEFT: Manny with actor Steven Seagal and Valerie Gonzales, President of MP Productions.

Manny and Jinkee escorted into the arena by Governor Chavit Singson (on Manny's right) and Edward Lura (on Jinkee's left).

Manny relaxing and singing inside his LA apartment.

Manny and his band perform at the grand opening of Island Pacific in Canoga Park.

Manny and Lito Camo in the Hollywood studio recording Manny's new album.

President Arroyo hands Manny his Official Master Sergeant Certificate as a reserve in the Philippine Army.

LEFT: Senior Master Sergeant Manny Pacquiao in the Army's reserve force.

Manny Pacquiao proudly carried the Philippine flag in the Parade of Nations for the 2008 Olympics.

TOP: *Manny takes a hit from Morales.*

MIDDLE: *Manny lands signature left against Morales in 2005.*

LEFT: *Giving thanks after defeating Morales.*

Bob Arum, Manny, Marco Antonio Barrera and Oscar De La Hoya at Will to Win press conference.

BELOW: To generate crowd excitement, Manny's willing to take a punch from Barrera.

BOTTOM: But he's always willing to give it back!

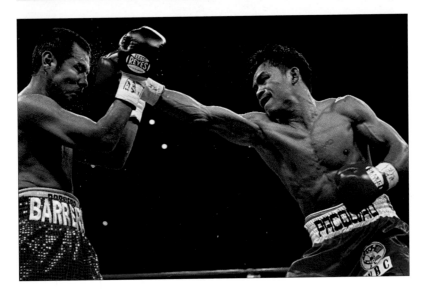

Unfinished business with Juan Manuel Marquez!

ABOVE:
Direct hit
to Marquez!

LEFT:
The business
is finished!

ABOVE: Diaz takes a painful hit!

LEFT:
And Diaz is down!

BELOW:
A win over Diaz!

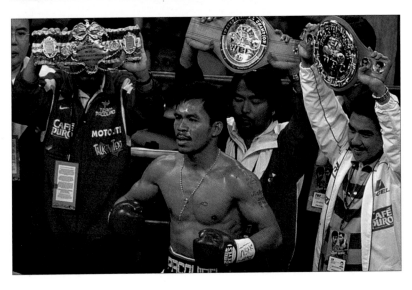

LEFT: *Manny and Oscar face off after the weigh-in for the Dream Match.*

BELOW: *Manny pummels De La Hoya into the ropes.*

BOTTOM LEFT: *De La Hoya concedes.*

BOTTOM RIGHT: *Pacman tells De La Hoya, "You're still my idol."*

Freddie Roach, Micky Rourke, Manny, and Ricky Hatton at the Battle of East and West press conference.

Bob Arum and Manny sharing moments during the East vs West press tour.

LEFT: Manny proudly waves Philippine flag after TKO over Hatton.

TOP: *Michael Koncz, Attorney Jeng Gacal, Freddie Roach and Manny at the Fire Power press conference.*

MIDDLE: *Manny vs. Miguel Cotto. The fight lived up to the name of the event—Fire Power!*

RIGHT: *Manny makes History with Cotto defeat—7th belt in a different weight class!*

Manny talks about reform just days before the election for Congress.

	Maacim		Maacim		Maacim
CONGRESSMAN					
1. CHIONGBIAN	110	228	605		85
2. PACQUIAO	917	639	888	1639	594

ABOVE: *Election results being tallied at "The Pentagon"—Manny's political headquarters.*

LEFT: *The word coming to "The Pentagon" is that 50% of the vote is in and it's 3-1 in Manny's favor!*

Jinkee campaigning for Manny.

Manny sworn in as Congressman of Sarangani.

It's all worth it!

PHOTOGRAPHS BY GERMAN VILLASENOR.

passion for my people. I didn't go into office owing a fortune to special interest groups. I knew that by paying out of my own pocket, I would be able to always focus on what would be best for the masses and not just a few.

There were other concerns as well, including how I would mix boxing with the duties of being a congressman. I knew that my legislative duties wouldn't interfere with my boxing schedule. Bob told the press, "Manny keeps in great shape and congressmen in the Philippines don't exactly knock themselves out at work."

I'll leave that one to Bob, but I did have a nice laugh. It made me feel good that Bob thought I could do it all because my win in May is just a few months short of my November "titans clash" with undefeated American welterweight Floyd Mayweather.

After my defeat in 2007, it would have been easy, and maybe normal, to have forgotten any aspirations of public service. But I couldn't forget my people and where I had come from. I am not someone who takes no for an answer. I just knew I had to work harder, I had to be persistent and persevere and never give up.

Calvin Coolidge, the thirtieth president of the USA, has a great quote that's worth repeating: "Nothing in the world can take the place of persistence. Talent will not; nothing is more common than unsuccessful men with talent. Genius will not; unrewarded genius is almost a proverb. Education will not; the world is full of educated derelicts. Persistence and determination alone are omnipotent."

No truer words have ever been spoken.

I knew that I had months of serious training ahead of me for a fight that had a record-breaking $80 million purse. I also knew that there would be enough time to work on the issues for my people. Both are epic fights, and I have more than enough energy to defeat all the foes.

Now, I'm asked if my congressional seat is just one more stepping stone to someday becoming president of the Philippines. I won't shut that door. I know I'll never forget the moment when Bob burst into my room to tell me, "You won, Mr. Congressman!" He also did a nice little dance, which isn't Bob's usual way.

I guess this news even stunned him. Maybe one day Bob will burst through my door and say, "Congratulations, Mr. President!"

APPENDIX

APPENDIX

MANNY'S BOXING CAREER

Light Flyweight and Flyweight

Manny started his professional boxing career in 1995 when he was just 16 years of age and weighed only 106 pounds (light flyweight). His early fights took place in small local venues and were shown on Vintage Sports' *Blow By Blow*, an evening boxing show.

January 22, 1995: Manny' professional boxing debut, a four-round bout against Edmund "Enting" Ignacio, which Manny won via decision.

In 1996, Manny's weight increased from 106 to 113 pounds before he lost in his twelfth bout against Rustico Torrecampo via a third-round knockout. Manny failed to make the required weight, so he was forced to use heavier gloves than Torrecampo, thereby putting him at a disadvantage. Early in the third round he moved forward into an overhand left from Tor-recampo, flattening him instantly.

Shortly after the Torrecampo fight, Manny settled at 112 pounds, winning the WBC World Flyweight title (his first major boxing world title as well as the flyweight lineal title) over Chatchai Sasakul by way of knockout in the eighth round.

Manny loses the title in his second bout against Med-goen Singsurat—also known as Medgoen 3K Battery—in a third-round knockout.

Super Bantamweight

After his loss to Singsurat, Manny gained weight and went to the super bantamweight division of 122 pounds, where he picked up the WBC International Super Ban-tamweight title. He defended this title five times before his chance to fight for a world title.

June 23, 2001: His big break was against former IBF World Super Bantamweight champion, Lehlohonolo Ledwaba. Manny was a late replacement on two weeks' notice but won the fight by a TKO to become the new IBF World Super Bantamweight champion (his second major box-ing world title). The bout was held at the MGM Grand

Las Vegas, in Las Vegas, Nevada. He went on to defend this title four times.

Featherweight

November 15, 2003: Manny fights Marco Antonio Barrera at the Alamodome, in San Antonio, Texas. This was a fight that many considered to have defined his career. Manny was fighting at featherweight for the first time, and he defeated Barrera via technical knockout in the eleventh round. Although this bout was not recognized as a title fight by any sanctioning bodies, after his victory Manny was crowned *The Ring* magazine's World Featherweight Champion, and he held that title until 2005.

May 2004: Manny challenges Juan Manuel Márquez who, at the time, held both the World Boxing Association (WBA) and International Boxing Federation (IBF) World Featherweight titles. The fight took place at the MGM Grand Las Vegas, on May 8, 2004, and after twelve rounds the bout was scored a draw, which proved to be a controversial decision that outraged both camps. At the end of a very close fight, the final scores were 115–110 for Márquez, 115–110 for Manny, and 113–113. One of the judges (who scored the bout 113–113) later admitted to making an error on the scorecards, because he had scored the first round as "10–7" in favor of Manny instead of the standard "10–6" for a three-knockdown round. Both parties felt they had done enough to win the fight.

Super Featherweight

March 19, 2005: Manny moves up in weight class, from 126 to 130 pounds, in order to fight a Mexican legend and three-division world champion, Érik Morales. The fight took place at the MGM Grand Las Vegas. However, this time around, in his first fight at super featherweight, Manny loses the twelve-round match by a unanimous decision from the judges, with all three scoring the fight 115–113 for Morales.

September 10, 2005: Manny fights Héctor Velázquez at the Staples Center in Los Angeles, knocking Velázquez out in six rounds to capture the WBC International Super Featherweight title—which he went on to defend five times. That same day, his rival, Erik Morales, fought against Zahir Raheem. However, Morales gave a lackluster performance, losing to Raheem via unanimous decision.

January 21, 2006: The much-anticipated rematch between Manny and Morales happened at the Thomas and Mack Center in Las Vegas. Morales escaped being knocked

APPENDIX

down twice, once during the second round by holding onto the ropes, and once in the sixth round by falling on the referee's body. Manny eventually knocked Morales out in the tenth round, which was the first time Morales had been knocked out in his boxing career.

July 2, 2006: Manny successfully defends his WBC International Super Featherweight title at the Araneta Coliseum in Quezon City, Philippines, against Óscar Larios—a two-time super bantamweight champion—who had moved up two weight divisions in order to challenge Manny. Manny wins by a unanimous decision, knocking down Larios two times during the twelve-round bout. The three judges scored the fight at 117–110, 118–108, and 120–106, all in favor of Manny.

November 18, 2006: Manny fights Morales a third time (with the series tied 1–1) at the Thomas & Mack Center in Las Vegas to a near-record crowd of over 18,000. Manny defeated Morales in a third-round knockout.

December 2006: Manny is named by both HBO and *The Ring* magazine as the "Fighter of the Year." HBO dubbed him the most exciting fighter of the year.

April 14, 2007: After a failed promotional negotiation with

201

Marco Antonio Barrera's camp, Bob Arum chooses Jorge Solís as Manny's next opponent; the bout was held in San Antonio. In the sixth round of the bout, an accidental head-butt occurred, giving Manny a cut under his left eyebrow. The fight ended in the eighth round when Manny knocked Solis down twice. Solis barely beat the count after the second knockdown, causing the referee to stop the fight and award Manny the win via knockout. The victory raised Manny's win-loss-draw record to 44–3–2, with 34 knockouts.

June 2007: The long-awaited rematch with Marco Antonio Barrera occurs despite Manny being the number one contender for the super featherweight title of Juan Manuel Márquez. Manny defeats Barrera in their rematch in an easy unanimous decision. In the eleventh round, Manny's punch caused a deep cut below Barrera's right eye. Barrera retaliated with an illegal punch on the break that dazed Manny but also caused the referee to deduct a point from Barrera. Two judges scored the bout 118–109, whereas the third scored it 115–112.

Other Events

In *The Ring* magazine, Manny (45–3–2) remained at the top of the super featherweight division (130 pounds). He had been in the ratings for 108 weeks. Manny was also at number two in the pound-for-pound category behind former welterweight champion Floyd Mayweather, Jr.

November 13, 2007: Manny honored by the WBC as *Champ Emeritus* during its 45th Annual World Convention held at the Manila Hotel.

November 20, 2007: José Nuñez, manager of WBO Super Featherweight champion Joan Guzmán, accuses Bob Arum (Manny's manager) of evading a match between the two boxers to protect Manny.

March 15, 2008: In a rematch against Juan Manuel Márquez called "Unfinished Business," Manny wins a disputed split decision. The fight was held at the Mandalay Bay Resort and Casino in Las Vegas. With this victory, Manny won the WBC and *The Ring* World Super Featherweight belts (as well as the lineal junior lightweight title), making him the first Filipino to win three world titles from major sanctioning bodies in three different weight divisions (Manny was a former WBC World Flyweight champion and former IBF World Super Bantamweight champion). However, with his *The Ring* World Featherweight belt, Manny had *de facto* won four world titles in four different weight classes at this point. The fight was a close, hard-fought battle, during which both fighters received cuts. The decisive factor was a third-round knockdown, when Márquez was floored by a crushing left hook by Manny. At the end of the fight, the judges' scores were 115–112 for Manny, 115–112 for Márquez, and 114–113 for Manny. In the post-fight press conference, Márquez's camp called for an immediate rematch, offering a six-million-dollar guarantee to Manny for a rematch. However, Manny ruled out a third fight with Márquez, stating: "I don't think so. This business is over." The reason that Manny did not want a rematch is because he intended to move up to the lightweight division in order to challenge David Díaz, the reigning WBC World Lightweight champion at that time. Díaz won the majority decision over Ramón Montano that night as an undercard of the "Unfinished Business" fight.

July 2008: It was announced that Manny would be the flag bearer of the Philippines at the 2008 Summer Olympics. He became the first Filipino Olympic non-participant to be Team Philippines' flag bearer during the opening ceremonies at the Beijing National Stadium. Swimmer Miguel Molina, 2005 Southeast Asian Games' Best Male Athlete, yielded the honor to Manny upon Philippine President Gloria Macapagal-Arroyo's request to national sports officials of the Philippines at the 2008 Summer Olympics.

August 7, 2008: The 240-member House of Representatives of the Philippines issues a resolution recognizing Manny as "a people's champ for his achievements and in appreciation of the honor and inspiration he has been bringing . . . to the Filipino people."

Lightweight

June 28, 2008: Manny defeats David Díaz in a ninth-round knockout at the Mandalay Bay Resort and Casino in Las Vegas, becoming the WBC World Lightweight champion. With this victory, Manny became the only Filipino and Asian boxer to win five world titles in five different weight classes. He also became the first Filipino fighter to ever win a world title at lightweight. During the fight, which Manny dominated, Díaz was cut badly on his right eye in the fourth round. After the bout, Díaz acknowledged Manny's superior hand speed, stating: "It was his speed. It was all his speed. I could see the punches perfectly, but he was just too fast." Bob Arum reported that the fight had made $12.5 million (250,000 pay-per-view subscriptions at $50 each), earning Díaz his best payday ever of $850,000, while Manny earned at least $3 million. Official records revealed an attendance of 8,362 (out of a maximum capacity of 12,000). Holding both the WBC World Super Featherweight and World Lightweight titles following

the win, Manny decided to vacate his super featherweight title in July 2008.

Welterweight

December 6, 2008: Manny moved up to the welterweight division in order to face six-division world
champion Oscar De La Hoya at the MGM Grand Las
Vegas. The fight, dubbed "The Dream Match," was
scheduled as a twelve-round, non-title fight contested
at the 147-pound welterweight limit. Although Manny
went into the fight widely recognized as the leading
pound-for-pound boxer in the world, some boxing
pundits had speculated that 147 pounds could be too
far above his natural weight against the larger De La
Hoya. However, Manny proved the critics wrong and
dominated the fight, and after eight rounds De La
Hoya's corner was forced to throw in the towel,
awarding Manny a technical knockout. Manny was
ahead on all three judges' scorecards before the fight
ended, with two judges scoring the fight at 80–71 and
one scoring it at 79–72. Manny landed 224 out of 585
punches, while De La Hoya landed only 83 out of
402 punches. After the bout, Freddie Roach stated:
"We knew we had him after the first round. He had
no legs, he was hesitant and he was shot." The fight
would be De La Hoya's last, as he announced his re-

tirement from boxing shortly after. Tickets reportedly sold out just hours after they went on sale. The total gate revenue for the fight was said to be nearly $17 million, making it the second largest gate revenue in boxing history.

Light Welterweight

May 2, 2009: Manny fights at the light welterweight for the first time against Ricky Hatton at the MGM Grand Las Vegas, in a fight billed as "The Battle of the East and West." Manny won by a knockout to claim the IBO and *The Ring* World Light Welterweight titles (as well as the lineal light welterweight title). The fight was originally in jeopardy due to disputes with both camps over the fight purse money. Eventually, the money issue was settled and the fight went on as scheduled, aired by HBO. Manny started the fight strong, knocking down Hatton twice in the first round. In the second round Hatton seemed to have recovered, as he stalked Manny for most of the round. However, with less than ten seconds remaining in the second round, Hatton was knocked out cold by a sharp left hook, prompting the referee to award Manny the win by knockout (at 2:59 of the round). The knockout won Manny *The Ring* magazine's "Knockout of the Year for 2009" award.

Return to Welterweight

November 14, 2009: Manny defeats Miguel Cotto by a
technical knockout in the twelfth round at the MGM
Grand Las Vegas, in a fight billed as "Fire Power."
Manny dominated the fight, knocking Cotto down in
rounds three and four before the referee stopped the
fight at 0:55 of round twelve. With this victory, Manny
took the WBO World Welterweight title, to become the
first fighter in boxing history to win seven world titles in
seven different weight divisions. Manny also won the
first and special WBC Diamond Championship belt.
This belt was created as an honorary championship ex-
clusively to award the winner of a historic fight between
two high-profile boxers. After the fight, promoter Bob
Arum was quoted as saying, "Manny is the greatest
boxer I've ever seen, and I've seen them all, including
Ali, Hagler, and Sugar Ray Leonard." Miguel Cotto said
in a post-fight interview: "Miguel Cotto comes to boxing to fight the biggest names, and Manny is one of the
best boxers we have of all time." Cotto showed heart,
and fans regarded this as one of the year's best fights.
The fight generated 1.25 million buys and $70 million
in domestic pay-per-view revenue, making it the most
watched boxing event of 2009. The match also generated a live gate of $8.8 million from an official crowd
of 15,930.

Following Manny's victory against Cotto, there was much public demand for a fight between Manny (the number one pound-for-pound boxer) and Floyd Mayweather, Jr. (the number two pound-for-pound boxer). Manny reportedly agreed to fight Mayweather on March 13, 2010, for a split of $50 million up front. It was later agreed that the venue for the fight would be the MGM Grand Las Vegas. However, the bout was put in jeopardy due to disagreements about Olympic-style drug testing. The Mayweather camp wanted random blood testing by the United States Anti-Doping Agency, whereas Manny refused to have any blood testing within 30 days from the fight because he thought it would weaken him, but he was willing to have blood taken from him before the 30-day window as well as immediately after the fight.

January 7, 2010: The Pacquiao/Mayweather fight is officially cancelled after the two camps cannot agree to the testing process and protocols.

March 13, 2010: Manny retains his WBO World Welterweight belt by defeating Joshua Clottey at Texas Stadium in Dallas, Texas, in a unanimous decision. The judges scored the fight 120–108, 119–109, and 119–109, all in favor of Manny. Manny threw a total of 1,231 punches (a career high), but landed just 246, as most were blocked by Clottey's tight defense. Clottey threw a total of 399 punches, landing 108. The crowd of 50,994 represented the third largest crowd for an indoor fight in boxing history. Additionally, the bout drew 700,000 pay-per-view buys and earned $35.3 million in domestic revenue.

MANNY'S POLITICAL CAREER

July 2006: Manny goes to the commission on elections office to file for official transfer of his residency from General Santos City to Manila, where he owns a condominium unit. He was accompanied by Ali Atienza, son of Manila Mayor Lito Atienza, fueling speculation that he planned to run for vice mayor of Manila. When asked about his political plans, he said he was still undecided and was concentrating on his boxing career.

February 12, 2007: Manny officially announces his run for a seat in the House of Representatives in the May 2007 legislative election as a candidate of the Liberal Party, aiming to represent the 1st District of South Cotabato. An ardent supporter of President Gloria Macapaga-Arroyo, Manny stated that he was persuaded to run by local officials of General Santos City, who hoped he would act as a bridge between their interests and the national government. Although he did not win the election, his incumbent opponent, Rep. Darlene Antonino-Custodio, was gracious in her post-election comments, stating, "More than anything, I think, people weren't prepared to lose him as their boxing icon."

September 2008: Manny is sworn in as a member of Kabalikat ng Malayang Pilipino (Kampi), a pro-administration political party.

In May 2010 Manny ran for and won the congressional seat of the Sarangani province against the founder's scion of that province in the Philippine general election. Manny is a member of the Nacionalista Party, headed by Manny Villar. Villar said arrangements was made to accommodate Manny's People's Champ Movement in a coalition with the Nacionalista Party for the May 2010 local elections in Sarangani.

MANNY IN POPULAR CULTURE

June 21, 2006: *Manny: The Movie*, a film based on Manny's life, is released, featuring Filipino actor Jericho Rosales as Manny and directed by Joel Lamangan.

2008: Manny stars with Ara Mina and Valerie Concepcion in *Anak ng Kumander*.

December 25, 2009: Manny stars in the superhero/comedy film entitled *Wapakman*, which was released as an entry to the 2009 Metro Manila Film Festival.

Manny is featured in the boxing video games *Fight Night Round 2*, *Fight Night Round 3*, and *Fight Night Round 4*. EA Sports released a limited edition demo of *Fight Night Round 4*, featuring Manny and Ricky Hatton prior to their fight.

Manny is the first Filipino athlete to appear on a postage stamp.

With his popularity, various business sectors have solicited Manny's help in endorsing their products through commercial advertisements in print and in broadcast media. These include detergents, medicines, foods, garments, telecommunications, and even a political ad for Chavit Singson during the May 14, 2007, elections. His most acclaimed commercials yet were for Nike's "Fast Forward" campaign (alongside Kobe Bryant, Maria Sharapova, Roger Federer, Cristiano Ronaldo, and Liu Xiang) and for San Miguel Beer with Jet Li and Érik Morales.

September 2007: Manny signs with GMA Network as an actor.

December 17, 2007: Manny tapes his first episode of *Pinoy Records*. His projects with the network included *Totoy Bato* and the sitcom *Show Me Da Manny*, where his mother, Dionesia, also appeared.

Manny and American actor Sylvester Stallone are discussing plans to do a feature film on Manny's life/autobiography. Stallone has stated his interest in doing a movie with Manny, who he said will be his co-star. This film would be Manny's big break to the American audience and American mainstream.

Manny was named by *Time* magazine as one of the world's most influential people for 2009 for his exploits in boxing and his influence among the Filipino people. Manny also appeared on the cover of *TIME* magazine Asia. He became the sixth Filipino to grace the cover of this prestigious magazine, after former Philippine presidents Manuel Quezon, Ramon Magsaysay, Ferdinand Marcos, Corazon Aquino and Filipino actress and environmentalist, Chin Chin Gutierrez.

Manny was named by *Forbes* magazine in its annual Celebrity 100 list for the year 2009, joining Hollywood actress Angelina Jolie and fellow athletes Tiger Woods and Kobe Bryant. *Forbes* also listed Manny as the world's sixth-highest-paid athlete with a total of $40 million from the second half of 2008 to the first half of 2009.

Manny won the 2009 ESPY Awards for the best fighter category, beating fellow boxer Shane Mosley and Brazilian mixed martial arts fighter Lyoto Machida.

November 2008: Manny was featured on the cover of *Reader's Digest* Asia in a seven-page story that was written about him.

MANNY'S PROFESSIONAL BOXING RECORD
Summary:51 Wins (38 knockouts, 13 decisions);
3 Defeats (2 by knockout, 1 by decision), 2 Draws

Result	Opponent	Type	Round	Date	Location
Win	Clottey	Decision	12	3/13/10	Texas Stadium
Win	Cotto	TKO	12	11/14/09	MGM Grand/Las Vegas
Win	Hatton	KO	2	5/2/09	MGM Grand/Las Vegas
Win	De La Hoya	KO	8	12/6/08	MGM Grand/Las Vegas
Win	Diaz	TKO	9	6/28/08	Mandalay Bay/Las Vegas
Win	Marquez	Decision	12	3/15/08	Mandalay Bay/Las Vegas
Win	Barrera	Decision	12	10/6/07	Mandalay Bay/Las Vegas
Win	Solis	KO	8	4/14/07	Alamodome/San Antonio
Win	Morales	KO	3	11/18/06	Thomas-Mark Ctr/Las Vegas
Win	Larios	Decision	12	7/2/06	Araneta Coliseum/Philippines
Win	Morales	TKO	10	1/21/06	Thomas-Mark Ctr/Las Vegas
Win	Velasquez	TKO	6	9/10/05	Staples Center/Los Angeles
Loss	Morales	Decision	12	3/19/05	MGM Grand/Las Vegas
Win	Thawatchai	TKO	4	12/11/04	Fort Bonifacio/Philippines
Draw	Marquez	Draw	12	5/8/04	MGM Grand/Las Vegas
Win	Barrera	TKO	11	11/15/03	Alamodome/San Antonio
Win	Lucero	KO	3	7/26/03	Olympic Auditorium/LA
Win	Yeshmagambetov	TKO	5	3/15/03	Rizal Park/Philippines
Win	Rakkiatgym	KO	1	10/26/02	Rizal Memorial/Philippines
Win	Julio	TKO	2	6/8/02	The Pyramid/Memphis, TN

Draw	Sanchez	Draw	6	11/10/01	Graham Audit/San Francisco
Win	Ledwaba	TKO	6	6/23/01	MGM Grand/Las Vegas
Win	Sakmuangklang	TKO	6	4/28/01	Kidapawan City, Philippines
Win	Senrima	TKO	5	2/24/01	Manila, Philippines
Win	Hussein	TKO	10	10/14/00	Ynares Center, Philippines
Win	Chae	TKO	1	6/28/00	Araneta Coliseum/Philippines
Win	Barotillo	KO	4	3/4/00	Aquino Stadium/Philippines
Win	Jamili	KO	2	12/18/99	Elorde Sports Complex/Philippines
Loss	Singsurat	KO	3	9/17/99	Thailand
Win	Mira	TKO	4	4/24/99	Araneta Coliseum/Philippines
Win	Makelim	TKO	3	2/20/99	Kidapawan City, Philippines
Win	Sasakul	KO	8	12/4/98	Thailand
Win	Terao	TKO	1	5/18/98	Tokyo, Japan
Win	Ohyuthanakorn	KO	1	12/6/97	Koronadal City, Philippines
Win	Magramo	Decision	10	9/13/97	Cebu City, Philippines
Win	Chockvivat	KO	5	6/26/97	Mandaluyong City, Philippines
Win	Austria	TKO	6	5/30/97	Davao City, Philippines
Win	Lee	KO	1	4/24/97	Makati City, Philippines
Win	Luna	KO	1	3/3/97	Muntinlupa City, Philippines
Win	Lee	TKO	2	12/28/96	Muntinlupa City, Philippines
Win	Gala	TKO	2	7/27/96	Mandaluyong City, Philippines
Win	Batiller	TKO	4	6/15/96	Mandaluyong City, Philippines
Win	Medina	TKO	4	5/5/96	Manila, Philippines
Win	Carillo	Decision	10	4/27/96	Manila, Philippines
Lose	Torrecampo	KO	3	2/9/96	Mandaluyong City, Philippines
Win	Torrejos	Decision	5	1/13/96	Paranaque City, Philippines
Win	Toyogon	Decision	10	12/9/95	Mandaluyong City, Philippines
Win	Fernandez	TKO	3	11/11/95	Mandaluyong City, Philippines
Win	Mendones	TKO	2	10/21/95	Palawan, Philippines
Win	Laroa	Decision	8	10/7/95	Makati City, Philippines
Win	Rocil	KO	3	9/16/95	Mandaluyong City, Philippines
Win	Simbajon	Decision	6	8/3/95	Mandaluyong City, Philippines
Win	Decierto	TKO	2	7/1/95	Mandaluyong City, Philippines
Win	Palma	Decision	6	5/1/95	Cavite City, Philippines
Win	Montejo	Decision	4	3/18/95	Mindoro Occidental, Philippines
Win	Enting	Decision	4	1995	Mindoro Occidental, Philippines

TITLES

Major

WBC World Flyweight champion

IBF World Super Bantamweight champion

The Ring World Featherweight champion

WBC World Super Featherweight champion

The Ring World Super Featherweight champion

WBC World Lightweight champion

The Ring World Junior Welterweight champion

WBO World Welterweight champion

Minor

IBO World Light Welterweight champion

Lineal Championship

World Flyweight champion

World Featherweight champion

World Junior Lightweight champion

World Junior Welterweight champion

Regional

OPBF Flyweight champion

WBC International Super Bantamweight champion

WBC International Super Featherweight champion

RECOGNITIONS

2000–09 Boxing Writers Association of America Fighter of the Decade

2000–09 Philippine Sportswriters Association Athlete of the Decade

2000–09 HBO Fighter of the Decade

2000–09 The SweetScience.com Fighter of the Decade

2006, 2008, and 2009 *The Ring* Fighter of the Year

2006, 2008, and 2009 Boxing Writers Association of America Fighter of the Year

2006 and 2008 SecondsOut.com Fighter of the Year

2008 and 2009 *The Ring* No. 1 Pound-for-Pound (year-end)
Five-time PSA Sportsman of the Year

2008 University Athletic Association of the Philippines

(UAAP) Honorary Award for Sports Excellence

2008 and 2009 BoxingScene.com Fighter of the Year

2008 *Sports Illustrated* Boxer of the Year

2008 and 2009 TheSweetScience.com Boxer of the Year

2008 and 2009 WBC Boxer of the Year

2008 Yahoo Sports Fighter of the Year

2008 and 2009 ESPN Star's Champion of Champions

2009 ESPN Fighter of the Year
2009 ESPN Knockout of the Year

2009 ESPY Awards Best Fighter

2009 *TIME* 100 Most Influential People (Heroes & Icons Category)

2009 *TIME Magazine* Asia cover for November 16, 2009 issue

2009 *Forbes Magazine* Celebrity 100 (ranked 57th)

2009 *Sports Illustrated* Fighter of the Year

2009 *The Ring Magazine* Knockout of the Year

2009 World's Greatest Ever Featherweight

2009 World's Greatest Ever (ranked 2nd *The Ring* Light Welterweight Champion: May 2, 2009 to Present

WBO Welterweight Champion: November 14, 2009 to Present

ACKNOWLEDGMENTS

THIS BOOK WAS WRITTEN as a part of my life to hopefully provide some inspiration and guidance to other people. It was purposefully written to help people understand how important spiritual guidance is, how important good decisions are, and how important it is to stay positive in your life. But, as important as any of these teachings are, the one quality of life that stands at the top is having quality friends surround you. Many people helped make this book possible, and I am grateful for every one of you and for your contribution.

First of all, I would like to offer this book to God, my Creator. Thank you Father for your gift of life and love....for always keeping me safe and secure...for being there when I needed you...for all the blessings you have given me and for choosing me to glorify you.

I would not be where I am now, were it not for the help and guidance of the following people during the early years of my boxing career. My heartfelt gratitude to Ambo Pablo & family, Polding Corea, Eling Alberto, Rey Golingan, Dizon Cordero & family, Zardo Mejia & family, Nanay Parcon &

family, Ador Balagbagan, Peewee Velasquez, Mario Suma-linog, Baby Tinagsa, Totong Vargas, Moi Lainez, Lito Mondejar and most specially to Rod Nazario.

To Gov. Chavit Singson, thank you for enlightening me with your worldly wisdom and outlook in life. I will always remain your humble and grateful friend.

To Mayor Lito Atienza, who is almost like a father to me. I am very thankful for all your unsolicited support and sound advise especially when it comes to my personal relationship with my wife and children. You have instilled in me the values of raising a loving, caring and God-fearing family.

To my *compadres*, Franklin "Jeng" Gacal and Eric Pineda (Batman & Robin of Team Pacquiao): thank you for your perseverance and for playing a very important role into making this book a reality.

To CHP International, which includes Curtis Cheaney, Howard Tong, Peter Phan and Henry Wang. I am so proud that all of you became part of the team to help put this whole book deal together, and to see it through all the way to the end. Howard, thank you for your faith on the book project, and for your "make-it-happen" business acumen. Peter and Henry, thank you for looking after my best interest, and for your unwavering commitment. Curtis, thank you for always staying positive, and for your persistence to get the job done. Peter Hayes, thank you for reading the manuscript over and over until you felt things were good enough for the readers to understand my life; and for your overall support to ensure the success of this book deal.

To Timothy James, thank you for envisioning what this book could be, for never giving up and for spending so much time and effort gathering the content, as well as putting my stories together for all to read. Thank you also to your assistant, Ed Palileo.

To the rest of Team Pacquiao, special thanks to Wakee Salud, Winchell Campos, Joe Ramos, Edward Lura, Jayke Joson, Aplas Fernandez, Carlos Homo, Jojo Sta, Teresa, Bren Evangelio, Rob Peters, Joseph Jose, Archie Banas, Bernie Torres, Danny Halibas, Jun Regalado, Jay Conte, Jovi Halog, Jing Oliva, Alex Oreto, Ping Nepomoceno, Jimmy Zuno, Ben Delgado, Pren Encarnacion, Mike Quidilla, Dr. Alan Recto, Dr. Ed dela Vega, Sonny Garcia and Warren Tojong.

Mike Koncz, thank you for doing everything that I asked you to do and for your persistence.

David Dunham, thank you for patiently waiting eighteen months to start working on this book. I hope I have done Dunham Books proud, as you have done me proud. Your work ethic is second-to-none. Cindy Pearlman and Emily Prather, thank you both for putting your great touches on the final product. And Mary Sue Englund: thank you for desiging a gorgeous package, both the cover and the interior.

Bob Arum, what can I say? You know me as well as anyone. You are not just my promoter but also one of my closest friend and confidant. You are a tireless inspiration of what a man should be. Thank you for helping me in my life, with my family and for always being there when I need you. I could not have made this journey in life without you.

Most importantly, thank you very much to my boxing team headed by my dear friend and boxing coach, Freddie Roach who is ably assisted by my childhood buddy, Buboy Fernandez, together with Alex Ariza and Nonoy Neri. All of you gentlemen played a major role in my quest to become one of the best boxers in history. I owe a great part of my success in the ring to you guys. Cheers!

Thank you also to my jogging partner and loyal dog, Pacman.

If I accidentally left anyone out—a special thanks to you as well!

Of course, I sincerely thank my parents, Daddy Rosalio and Mommy Dionisia, for bringing me into this world and for raising me as a good Christian. To my siblings, Bobby, Rogelio and Isidra, thank you always for your love and concern for my wellbeing. To my wife's family, namely: Daddy Nestor, Mommy Rosalina, Haydee, Janet, Russell and Dondon, thank you for accepting me for who I am and for who I am not.

To my children Emmanuel, Michael, Princess and Queenie; they mean the world to me and without them my world would not be complete. I love you all from the bottom of my heart.

And last, but not least, to my dear lovely wife, Jinkee, who is my source of strength and stability, thank you for your unconditional love and for always being there by my side through thick or thin. I love you very much!